FROM SOUL TO SELF

'*From Soul to Self* is a fascinating survey of thought about the
Soul/Body relationship. It ranges boldly from Shamanism
and ancient Philosophy through Greek Christianity to
Augustine and Descartes to the latest thinking in science
and philosophy. It makes one vividly aware of the complexity of issues involved.'

Paul Badham, *University of Wales*

From Soul to Self takes us on a fascinating journey through philosophy, theology, religious studies, and physiological sciences. Each
of the essays, drawing from a number of different fields, focuses on
the idea of the soul and of our sense of ourselves. The contributors
are leading experts from a number of distinct fields, including
Richard Sorabji from Ancient Philosophy, Anthony Kenny from
Medieval Philosophy, Susan Greenfield from neuroscience, and
Kallistos Ware from Theology.

A stellar line-up of authors explore the relationship between a
variety of ideas that have arisen in philosophy, religion and science,
each idea seeking to explain why we think we are as individuals
somehow distinct and unique.

M. James C. Crabbe is Professor of Protein Biochemistry, and Head
of the Division of Cell and Molecular Biology at the University of
Reading. He is also a fellow of Wolfson College, Oxford.

FROM SOUL
TO SELF

Edited by
M. James C. Crabbe

London and New York

First published 1999
by Routledge
11 New Fetter Lane, London EC4P 4EE

Simultaneously published in the USA and Canada
by Routledge
29 West 35th Street, New York, NY 1001

Routledge is an imprint of the Taylor & Francis Group

Typeset in Garamond by
Florence Group, Stoodleigh, Devon
Printed and bound in Great Britain by
Biddles Ltd, Guildford and King's Lynn

British Library Cataloguing in Publication Data
A catalogue record for this book is available from the British Library

Library of Congress Cataloging in Publication Data
From soul to self/edited by M. James C. Crabbe.
p.   cm
Includes bibliographical references and index.
1.   Soul–History. 2.   Self (Philosophy)–History.
I. Crabbe, M. James C.
BD421.F76 1999-01-18   98–41840
128'.1–dc21   CIP

ISBN 0–415–17117–2 (hbk)
ISBN 0–415–17118–0 (pbk)

CONTENTS

FIGURES

CONTRIBUTORS

M. James C. Crabbe is Professor of Protein Biochemistry, and Head of Cell and Molecular Biology at the University of Reading, and a Fellow of Wolfson College, Oxford. His research interests centre on protein structure and function in health and disease, and he has over 130 publications in books and refereed journals, as well as being the author of a suite of computer programs for molecular modelling in chemistry and biology. He is a member of the MRC Advisory Board, a member of the Council of Biochemical Society, and Editor-in-chief of the journal *Computers and Chemistry*. In addition, he has produced a number of records of classical music, including 'The Sound of the Georgian Piano' for RCA.

Susan Greenfield has held fellowships in the Department of Physiology, Oxford, the Collège de France, Paris and the NYU Medical Center, New York. In 1985 she was appointed University Lecturer in Synaptic Pharmacology and Fellow and Tutor in Medicine, Lincoln College, Oxford. Subsequently she has also held a Visiting Research Fellowship at the Institute of Neuroscience, La Jolla, USA, and was the 1996 Visiting Distinguished Scholar, Queens University, Belfast. In 1994 she was the first woman to be invited to give the Royal Institution Christmas lectures and has subsequently made a wide range of broadcasts on television and radio. The title of Professor of Pharmacology was conferred in 1996. In 1997 she was awarded an Honorary DSc by Oxford Brookes University, and received Honorary DSc degrees in 1998 from the University of St Andrew's and Exeter University. She became Director of The Royal Institution of Great Britain in 1998.

Sir **Anthony Kenny** was until recently Warden of Rhodes House, Oxford, and a Professorial Fellow of St John's College, Oxford.

From 1964 to 1978 he was Fellow and Tutor in Philosophy at Balliol College, and was Master of that College from 1978 to 1989. His many published works include *Action, Emotion and Will* (1963), *Descartes* (1968), *Wittgenstein* (1973), *Will, Freedom and Power* (1975), *The Aristotelian Ethics* (1978), *Freewill and Responsibility* (1978), *Aristotle's Theory of the Will* (1979), *The Legacy of Wittgenstein* (1984), *The Metaphysics of Mind* (1989), *Aristotle on the Perfect Life* (1992) and *Aquinas on Mind* (1993). He edited *The Oxford Illustrated History of Western Philosophy* (1994). He has been visiting professor at a number of universities in North America and holds nine honorary doctorates from universities in Britain, Ireland and the United States. Elected a Fellow of the British Academy in 1974 he served as President for the period 1989–93. He was Chairman of the British Library Board from 1993–6.

Gary Matthews is Professor of Philosophy at the University of Massachusetts, Amherst. He is author of *Thought's Ego in Augustine and Descartes* (1992), *The Philosophy of Childhood* (1994), as well as the forthcoming book *Socratic Perplexity and the Nature of Philosophy* (1999). He is the editor of *The Augustinian Tradition* (1998).

Peter Rivière is Professor of Social Anthropology at the University of Oxford and a Fellow of Linacre College. His lifetime research interest has been the native people of Amazonia with particular reference to the north-eastern part of the region where he has undertaken numerous field trips. His attention has mainly focused on kinship, social and symbolic classification, mythology, the nature of personhood (including ideas about conception and death), and causality. His main published monographs are *Marriage Among the Trio* (1969), *The Forgotten Frontier* (1972), *Individual and Society in Guiana* (1984), and *Absent-minded Imperialism* (1995).

Richard Sorabji was brought up in Oxford, so had great pleasure in returning as a Supernumerary Fellow to Wolfson College. In the interim, he taught first at The Sage School of Philosophy in Cornell University and since 1970 in the Philosophy Department at King's College, London, where he is a Professor of Ancient Philosophy. His books include a trilogy on physics (*Necessity, Cause and Blame*; *Time, Creation and the Continuum*; *Matter, Space and Motion*) and a planned trilogy on mind and ethics (*Animal*

Minds and Human Morals; *From Emotion to Temptation* (forth-coming); and a next book on *Ancient Concepts of the Self*). He was for five years Director of the Institute of Classical Studies in London, and is currently holder of one of the British Academy's two Research Professorships. He is a fellow of the British Academy, foreign honorary member of the American Academy of Arts and Sciences and a C.B.E.

Galen Strawson is Fellow and Tutor in Philosophy at Jesus College, Oxford and Lecturer in Philosophy at the University of Oxford. He is an editorial consultant at the Times Literary Supplement. In 1993 he was a Visiting Fellow at the Research School of Social Sciences, Australian National University, and in 1997 he was a Visiting Professor at New York University. He is the author of *Freedom and Belief* (1986), *The Secret Connexion: Realism, Causation, and David Hume* (1989), *Mental Reality* (1994), and is writing a book about the self.

Kallistos Ware is Fellow and Tutor at Pembroke College, Oxford, as well as being Bishop of Diokleia in the Greek Orthodox Church. He has published many articles in the *Journal of Ecclesiastical History* and the *Journal of Theological Studies*, in addition to studies on the spirituality of the 'Philokalia'. He has been a Jane Eliza Proctor Visiting Fellow at Princeton University.

PREFACE

Implicit in the title of this book is a journey; or, perhaps more accurately, an exploration. Travel into unexplored territory requires some assistance, and this volume aims to act as a guide book to an area which links philosophy, theology, religious studies, history, anthropology and physiological sciences. It is a journey travelled both by individuals and by societies made up of those individuals. It is not, however, a simple journey, a progression from A to B, starting with the soul and ending at the self. Rather, the chapters in this book are a series of rigorous discussions of ideas of the soul and of our sense of ourselves, written from different viewpoints. They are comments on changing perceptions, of ourselves as individuals and of our capacities for living.

The book had its origins in a series of lectures given at Wolfson College, Oxford, in 1996, as one of the annual Wolfson College Lecture Series. Each chapter is written by one of the distinguished speakers who were asked to give a general survey of their topic to an audience who were not specialists in the lecturer's own field of study. The essays are based on those lectures, but with many new additions and cross-references. They aim to appeal to the general reader and specialist alike; to philosophers, historians, scientists, anthropologists and students of religions of the world. While most chapters contain a list of references, there is also a select bibliography for those who wish to read further about any aspect of the subjects covered in this book. I hope this volume can convey something of the *frisson* and excitement which the speakers succeeded in conveying to their audience, both during the lectures, and afterwards at the discussion sessions.

Apart from the authors themselves, I am indebted to the President of Wolfson College, Sir David Smith and to his wife, the members of the Academic Policy Committee at Wolfson, Professor Richard

Sorabji, Professor Richard Gombrich, Dr Michael Argyle, Dr John Ashton and Dr David Edge for their excellent advice, and particularly to a former vicegerent of the College, Professor Jim Kennedy and to his successor, Dr John Penny, who have given their unfailing support and encouragement.

M. James C. Crabbe

1

INTRODUCTION

M. James C. Crabbe

Nature that fram'd us of four elements,
Warring within our breasts for regiment,
Doth teach us all to have aspiring minds:
Our soul, whose faculties can comprehend
The wondrous Architecture of the world . . .
Still climbing after knowledge infinite,
And always moving as the restless Spheres.
(Conquests of Tamburlaine, Christopher Marlowe (1564–93))

A high degree of order is one of the basic characteristics of life.
Order exists not only at levels which we may perceive, for example
in the fingers on a hand, but also at levels which we cannot perceive
without aid, such as in the organization of cells within the tissues
of the body. This organization is based on a hierarchy of structural
levels, each level building on the one below it, just as levels within
society are ultimately built upon the individual. Atoms, the chemical building blocks of nature, are ordered into complex biological
molecules such as proteins and nucleic acids. As we step up the
hierarchy of order, novel properties emerge that were not present
at simpler levels of organization. These emergent properties result
from interactions between components that make the whole greater
than the sum of the parts. Unique properties arise from how parts
are arranged and interact, not from supernatural powers.

But is this true for the highest properties of the mind? Dualism
– the idea that there are two worlds – maintains that there is the
physical world, which contains matter and all the tangible components of the Universe, and another psychical world. In the latter
world, mental states and events are inaccessible to observation. The
essence of mind is consciousness, and the relationship between
mental phenomena and physical phenomena has exercised thinkers

1

over many centuries; recently it has become known as the mind–body problem. For those seeking a connection between the mental and physical worlds, then there they may find the soul. The German philosopher Hegel (1770–1831) regarded the soul as the lowest, sensory manifestation of the spirit in its connection with matter. The *Oxford Dictionary of Philosophy* defines the soul as: 'The immaterial "I" that possesses conscious experience, controls passion, desire, and action, and maintains a perfect identity from birth (or before) to death (or after).'

One may view the soul from a number of perspectives; philosophical, historical, theological and scientific. None of the chapters in this volume aims to be completely comprehensive; rather, they seek to give a flavour of the important interdisciplinary studies that make up our understanding of the nature of the soul. This interdisciplinary approach has a long and well-attested provenance. The early masters at Oxford, many of whom had studied in Paris, brought together interests in theology, philosophy and natural science. Greek and Arabic sources of philosophy, natural science and medicine had come into the West in translation from about the second half of the twelfth century, often via Spain, where the reconquest of Toledo by the Christians in 1085 opened the way for access to material preserved and developed by Islamic scholars. One item of special interest to the medieval Latin-speaking scholars was the nature and power of the soul. Ideas on the soul were often derived from the works of the Greeks Heraclitus (*fl.* 504 BC), Socrates (470–399 BC), Plato (427–347 BC), and Aristotle (384–322 BC), and from Arabic sources such as the De anima of Avicenna.

Adam of Buckfield (*fl.* 1238–1278) is an interesting example of an Oxford master of the mid-thirteenth century; his intelligent expositions were widely appreciated at the time, and his commentaries anticipated those of Thomas Aquinas. The Oxford master propounded the view that the intellective soul of man was separable from matter, and was therefore of a different nature from lower forms, which also animated man. Arguments continued between theologians and philosophers as to whether there was a unified soul, or whether the intellective, sensitive and vegetative souls were distinct substances in man. These controversies have continued since medieval times; indeed they recur throughout this book, and in many manifestations.

Some of the questions being posed today may have changed in form, but not materially in substance, from those discussed by earlier philosophers. Do we have souls? Are souls sources of life or of mind? If souls exist are they material or immortal? Can the soul be distinguished from the self? What criteria do we use for individual identity? Can animal souls be distinguished from human souls? How much do we need a concept of the soul in order to fulfil ourselves as human beings?

These questions lead naturally to a number of themes which appear, like philosophical leitmotivs, throughout this book. Four major themes, which are orchestrated in different ways by the authors, deal with process, language, maps and consciousness. These four themes may be summarized in four questions. Is the soul a thing or a process? Is there an asymmetry between language comprehension and production? Can the philosopher and the scientist provide valid maps of the mind? How much is the sense of self a product of conscious reasoning or of the imagination? The chapters in this volume also illustrate the point that philosophical, theological and scientific discussions on these and related issues are not merely of academic interest; they are useful both as guidelines for individual actions, and for mapping out areas for further study.

While each chapter is self-sufficient, a preliminary note on each may help the reader with some of the themes and topics discussed in the book. In Chapter 2, Richard Sorabji amplifies ideas on the soul and the self from the perspective of the Greek philosophers, from Plato and Aristotle in the fourth century BC to Plotinus and the later Neoplatonists of the fifth and sixth centuries AD. In the first section of his chapter, he discusses ideas of philosophers who initiated studies on what we might now consider as the relationships between the soul, the mind, and the brain. The soul was divisible into a number of forms; the intellective soul, the sensitive soul, the nutritive soul. Democritus (c. 460–c.371 BC), regarded the soul as something secondary to, and dependent upon, the body, while reducing its activity to mechanical or physico-chemical processes. The idea of an immortal soul was a subject for discussion, and often fitted in with the current religious and cosmological view. The atomists thought that the soul consisted of 'atoms' moving easily throughout the body, and that the soul was dispersed after death; part of the aim of this idea was to free men and women from a superstitious fearful belief in an afterlife involving punishment. Original views were often subject to distortion by later philosophers. For example, according to Aristotle, Alcmaeon (fifth century BC) held that the soul was immortal because it was like the immortals, insofar as it is always in motion; the divinities were always in constant motion – the moon, the sun, the stars and the whole heaven. Later Christian theological ideas were to build on much of the earlier Greek philosophical concepts. In the second section of his chapter, Sorabji develops a number of classical ideas of the self, including those of personality and personal identity over time, that are also discussed in the final chapter by Galen Strawson. In Chapter 3 Anthony Kenny reviews the writings of Aquinas on the soul. While St Thomas Aquinas interpreted Greek philosophy in accord with Christian teaching, he was no less a philosopher than Descartes (1596–1650) or Russell (1872–1970). In the medieval period, there was often a tension between the insights of natural knowledge derived from the natural cognitive powers of the intellect and the senses, and the insights into supernatural knowledge derived from (divine) revelation. Aquinas recognized the importance of the relationship between the intellect and the imagination. He developed a complicated map of the mind to help chart this relationship. The development of such a 'philosophical map' (and that of Aquinas was superior to that of many other philosophers) should be helpful if considered along with a 'scientific map', which could be produced using scientific scanning of individual neurone connections. An approach to the latter concept is developed further in the chapter by Susan Greenfield. Kenny believes that there is no separate self; rather that 'myself is just myself'. This notion is discussed in some detail in the chapters by Richard Sorabji and Galen Strawson.

In Chapter 4, Kallistos Ware, a Bishop in the Greek Orthodox Church, argues that many of the Early Fathers based their ideas on Greek philosophy, modified by Christian teaching. For some of them, the image, a starting point with potential, was not the same as the likeness, an actuality and an endpoint. Growth of man's soul, however it was constructed, and whichever part of the body – often the heart – it was associated with, was a journey from the image (of God) to the likeness (of God), and this growth could continue throughout eternity. Such growth – a process of rebirth – implies a process of progression, described by Sorabji as an attractive view of the immortal soul. Here we move into areas of mystery. Often it is difficult to draw the line between affirming mystery and talking nonsense. When does one cross the line? One of the tests may be in terms of prayer and worship, rather than of strict philosophy. Crossing a threshold into a religious space takes us beyond the rational need to manipulate dissect, calibrate or observe. In the words of the sociologist, the Revd. Professor David Martin:

Across that threshold observation gives place to insight, object becomes emblem, and the givens of analysis manifest themselves as pure gift. In such space a sign language focuses vision, because without focus vision vanishes, though it is not its nature to impose itself in the way propositions and observations impose themselves. Signs invite us to *dis*cover or *un*cover what is meant by disintegration and integrity, frustration and fulfillment, chaos and order, evil and good, scarcity and plenitude, absence and presence. Horizons open up, with pointers of deformation and markers of transformation
(From a sermon delivered at Jesus College, Cambridge)

We leave the confines of the literary and civilized traditions of the Western world in Chapter 5, where anthropologist Peter Rivière describes some of the beliefs relevant to the soul held by various peoples of South America, particularly those people living around the Amazon Basin. His ethnographic work draws out many philosophical parallels between cultures like the Trio people in Brazil and Surinam without any historical continuity, and cultures with historical traditions like our own in Europe. He also argues that there are parallels in ideas of 'consciousness and the soul' held by the Bororo peoples of Central Brazil and the Cashinahua peoples of Brazil and Peru, with our modern scientifically based views of human consciousness and the mind, as developed in the chapter by Susan Greenfield.

Similar parallels exist in other societies and with other religions; for example Buddhism. For the Buddhist, soul and self are (linguistically) identical, and denoted by the word ätman. Rebirth is also an important concept in Indian philosophy, the ätman undergoing a number of 'rebirths', or transmigrations, en route to attaining a pure goal:

Know thou the self (*ätman*) as riding in a chariot,
The body as the chariot.
Know thou the intellect (*buddhi*) as the chariot-driver,
And the mind as the reins.
The senses, they say, are the horses;
The objects of sense, what they range over.
The self combined with senses and mind
Wise men call 'the enjoyer'.
He, however, who has not understanding,

Who is unmindful and ever impure,
Reaches not the goal,
But goes on to rebirth [transmigration].
He, however, who has understanding,
Who is mindful and ever pure,
Reaches the goal
From which he is born no more
(*Katha Upanishad* II, 18–20.
8th–7th century BC)

As implied by many authors in this volume, the goal would be a rather unattractive one to us if it were simply frozen in time, and did not in itself involve progression or rebirth.

The Buddha was essentially a practical philosopher who got down to basic essentials of life without over-emphasizing metaphysical ideas. For the Buddha, the five 'bundles' (skandha) – aspects dealing with physical laws, sensations, apperceptions, volitions and consciousness (all ideas we come across in other chapters in this volume, from philosophers with very different traditions) were not *things* but *processes*, relevant to human experience. In Buddhism, the most important things go on in the mind. Rather than being a simple 'no soul doctrine', Buddhism implies that it is better to lose concern in one's self (soul) in concern for other suffering beings.

In Chapter 6, Gary Matthews discusses the ideas of animal souls in the writings of St Augustine (354–430 AD) and Descartes (1596–1650). Matthews develops the 'argument from analogy' in Augustine to arrive at the thesis: 'The mind of each of us know what a mind is simply and solely by knowing itself.' He then amplifies Descartes's argument for Dualism, and shows that Descartes's ideas are incompatible with a psychological continuity between humans and animals. In dualistic doctrines, such as Descartes's, the soul was looked on as something that has independent existence, that exists alongside the body. Descartes used language arguments to illustrate his theme, but neglects a key difference between linguistic comprehension and production. The Augustinian view of animal souls is more compatible with a continuity in the animal kingdom, rather than a single cut-off point between humans and the rest. The argument for continuity is also more in line with our understanding derived from current science, and these ideas are developed further in Chapter 7 by Susan Greenfield.

Greenfield argues that consciousness is a continuum, and while there is no 'conscious centre' that can be mapped specifically in the brain, imaging techniques show that there are hard-wired transient assemblies of neurones. If these assemblies can be correlated with conscious activity – or even shown to predict a form of it – then such maps could act as an 'underground map' or 'Rosetta stone' for relating mind and brain. Such ideas of transient connections have parallels with the concept of a 'soul of fire' of Heraclitus; that is something which is continuous, like a flame, but always changing in form. It might be argued that such a deterministic view of the soul leaves aside metaphysical considerations, and while it cannot yet explain concepts of will and free will, it has parallels with many ideas of the soul, from the early Greeks, through the Buddha, to modern tribes in South America.

In Chapter 8 by Galen Strawson, we come to a consideration of the self or rather, the sense we have of our own self. Such a sense transcends our cultural heritage, and Strawson argues that the 'mental self', while certainly not a mythical entity, is not continuous, but continually reborn. This disjunction has many parallels, not least with the transient connections and thought processes described in the previous chapter, based on physiological experimentation and imaging. Consciousness is therefore not so much a stream as a series of pools and rivulets, in 'perpetual flux and movement' (David Hume, 1711–76). Thus Hume's 'bundle' theory of the mind or self – that we have no reason to think in terms of a single unified self that owns a variety of experiences or states; we only have access to the succession of states themselves – was anticipated by Buddhism. Such an underlying principle for our sense of ourselves can then be modified to develop ourselves as outward manifestations, with many different conceptions. Thus the map of the mind we might arrive at would be of a multi-dimensional form; a series of lakes or pools connected by underlying flowing currents. In the words of Susan Greenfield: 'spatially multiple, yet effectively single – at any one time' (p. 112). Running through the many levels there would be a continuing consciousness (or sub-consciousness) that would emerge – either spontaneously or as a result of experience – at another level as a 'reborn' sense of the self.

2

SOUL AND SELF IN ANCIENT PHILOSOPHY

Richard Sorabji

Part I: Soul

Do we have a soul?

How many of us now believe we have souls? There are at least two reasons why we hesitate. First, we tend to think of the soul as something immortal, and in the English-speaking countries doubt has spread about immortality. Second, Descartes revised the Aristotelian concept of soul and marked the revision by switching to the word 'mind' (*mens*).[1] As a result all of us, I believe, would think we had minds, but many would doubt if we had souls.

What I want to say is that ancient concepts of soul were very various, and only some of them involved immortality. Among those which did not is Aristotle's biological concept of soul, which it would be hard to disagree with in its broad outlines. Other concepts connect soul with specifically mental functions, rather than with the full range of biological functions, and some of these too deny immortality. The question whether we have a soul might get a quite different answer, when we look at some of these concepts.

Given the variety of acceptable concepts, ancient philosophers had little motive to deny that we have souls. It has recently been argued, we shall see, that the Aristotelian Dicaearchus did not deny it.

Biological versus immortal and purely mental soul

According to Aristotle's biological conception, the soul is that set of capacities which distinguishes living from non-living things. Humans have the capacity to reason, to perceive and desire and to use food to grow to maturity, to maintain that structure and to

8

produce seed for the next generation. Animals lack the reasoning capacity, plants have only the nutritive capacity, which involves no mental functions at all.[2] That we have a soul, in the sense of having such capacities, is hardly to be denied.

Aristotle was retaining the view of his predecessors, Empedocles and Plato, that plants have souls. But Plato thought plants were sensitive, while Empedocles had gone further and believed he had once been incarnated as a bush.[3] Aristotle, Plato's pupil, is giving a new biological rationale to the belief in plant souls.

He also sought to define the various capacities which define life, an enterprise which still continues today. The capacity for growth in all biological species is not a mere capacity for increase in size through feeding, since even fires grow in that sense. Rather, the growth in question maintains a certain structure and size.[4] The human capacity for reason and rational belief is carefully distinguished[5] from the capacity of the lion to perceive that the ox is near and rejoice that he will have a meal.[6]

Aristotle also observes species to see where soul is to be found. He admits that we sometimes do not know how to classify species, because, for example, it is hard to tell whether sea anemones and sea squirts are sensitive.[7]

When Descartes claims to be revising Aristotle's idea of non-conscious nutritive souls, he ascribes it to 'the earliest men'. He seems to be unaware that it is an innovation of Aristotle's, and that the innovation, moreover, was rejected after Aristotle by Epicureans, Stoics, certain Pythagoreans, the Jewish Philosopher Philo and the Neoplatonist Porphyry, who all prefer to reject plant souls, rather than admit a type of soul with no mental functions.[8]

Slightly more controversial is Aristotle's view that the capacities *explain* animal movement, plant growth and so on.[9] Not that Aristotle fails to welcome physical explanations, but he thinks these explain in a different way, by showing how the capacities work.[10]

Immortal versus mortal soul

Aristotle thought the human soul mortal, but it has been said that the idea of its mortality was not explicitly expressed until the century before Aristotle, on an inscription commemorating the battle of Potidaea in 432 BC.[11] Before that in Homer, the soul, however, had a very dismal after life.[12] It has been said that this fits with the fact that most of the mental functions were associated with parts of the living body such as breath and lungs.[13] Thus immortality of soul did not in

Homer offer the continuance of full mental function and personality. Of course, many philosophers believed the soul to be immortal and gave it a full after life, a good number combining this with belief in reincarnation. The first philosophical questioning of the soul's immortality is articulated by Plato. He himself upholds, and makes Socrates uphold, immortality. But he puts into the mouth of Socrates' interlocutors the suggestion that the soul might be dependent on the body, like the harmony of a stringed instrument. It might be the harmony of the body, or the blend of qualities in the body.[14] The theory of the soul as bodily blend, and so perishable, was later endorsed by the Aristotelian Dicaearchus[15] and the Platonizing doctor Galen.[16] Although Galen professes ignorance whether there may also be a Platonic immortal soul,[17] his discussion leaves one thinking its existence would be a mystery. Other Aristotelians prefer to think that the soul is a capacity supervening on the bodily blend,[18] but this still leaves it perishable, as Aristotle had left it. The Epicureans make a special point of the soul being a collection of atoms dispersed at death. They do so for therapeutic reasons to which I shall come later. The Stoics think of soul as air and fire pervading our bodies with a special tension. Virtuous souls may have enough tension to hold together after death for varying amounts of time, but at latest until the next conflagration of the universe.[19]

Seven hundred and more years after Aristotle's death, the Neoplatonists wanted to harmonize Aristotle's views with Plato's, partly to ward off Christian charges of pagan self-contradiction. So they made out that he believed our rational soul was immortal after all. By an irony, this helped Thomas Aquinas to make Aristotle respectable for Christians, some sixteen hundred years after his death. But it was certainly not Aristotle's intention.[20]

Material versus immaterial soul; not correlated with mortal versus immortal

The Greeks did not at first find it easy to articulate the idea of things being immaterial, as appears in many contexts, for example in early discussions of vacuum, or of numbers. In Homer the soul that goes down to the house of Hades is visible, twitters, can sometimes be made to speak, but cannot be embraced any more than a dream or shadow.[21] Plato offers the first extensive discussion of the soul's immateriality in the *Phaedo*. Having argued that universals like equality are distinct form any of the physical objects which possess equality, he then claims that our soul is like these universals for example in not being perceptible by the senses.[22] But there is a striking compromise in Plato's conception. Although the soul is not a body, it can make spatial movements, movements which cannot be directly perceived, but which can be inferred. This is how the physical movements of music, rocking and dance can calm our souls, by altering their movements, and how the physical movements of childhood growth delay the acquisition of rational thought. If the circular movements of the rational part of the soul get distorted by poor use of reason we may be reincarnated as animals with a long snout, to house the distorted movements. Again we see the effect of circular movement in the world's soul, when we watch the stars go round.[23] Plato further makes Socrates joke that souls which have become too attached to bodily things in life can subsequently be seen as ghosts.[24]

The Neoplatonists thought that our souls, though immaterial, need a physical vehicle. The fleshly vehicle can be shed, and perhaps the vehicle made of *pneuma* or physical spirit, but not the luminous vehicle.[25]

Platonism was only one strand in Greek thought. Both Epicurus and the Stoics reverted to the early Greek conception of soul as a body, partly on the grounds that causal interaction can only be between bodies.[26] For Epicurus soul is a group of atoms,[27] for the Stoics spirit (*pneuma*) composed of air and fire.[28] The term 'spirit' (*pneuma*) did not at first imply immateriality, although that is how Christians eventually came to use it.[29] By earlier Greeks, it was used in the same way as 'animal spirits', 'methylated spirits', 'wines and spirits'.

Aristotle was as insistent as Plato that our soul is not an extended thing (a *megethos*).[30] But the sense of his idea is very different. Being a set of capacities, it is not a body, but is utterly dependent on body, and indeed on body of a particular type.[31] The same would be true of those who held that the soul was the blend of bodily qualities, or that it was a capacity supervening on that blend.

Augustine attacks both the idea that the soul is a body and the idea that it is a bodily blend (*temperatio*) or harmony (*compago*). He uses an argument later adapted by Descartes. We cannot doubt that we are alive, remember, understand, want, think, know and judge, for doubting would involve precisely these activities. Thus the soul knows itself with certainty and hence knows its essence (*substantia*) with certainty. But it is not certain whether it is material. So it is not. A further sign that it is not is the fact that it uses imagination to consider the various material things it fancies it might be. But

11

if it were one of these things, it would not need imagination, for nothing is more directly present to the soul than itself.[32]

Though denying that the soul is a blend, Augustine, following the Neoplatonist Porphyry, thinks it may enjoy a certain kind of blending (*unio inconfusa*) with the body. Porphyry had discussed the Stoic view that, in chemical combination, wine and water can get into the very same place as each other, and yet (this part is true) can be re-separated by an oil-drenched sponge. Porphyry denies this is possible for bodies. But for intelligibles like the soul, something analogous would be possible.[33]

There is no correlation between the issue of whether the soul is a body and whether it is mortal. Aristotle, Epicurus and the Stoics made it mortal, in spite of denying it was a body. Conversely, early views from Homer to the Presocratics tended to describe it as a body, yet Homer, the Pythagoreans and Empedocles particularly emphasised its immortality. The Stoics, we saw, consciously made the soul a body, yet allowed it to persist in some cases for a long time after death.

What does the human soul contain besides reason?

The relation of the soul to reason makes a big difference to how the soul is conceived. Plato in the *Phaedo* thinks of the soul as reason, though not as a mere information-processor, since in Plato reason always has its own pleasures and desires. In the *Republic*, Plato adds on two irrational parts of the soul, called by later thinkers the emotional part (*pathētikon*). One argument for this addition is that we sometimes have opposite wants and opposites cannot belong to a single unitary subject at the same time.[34] A later text of pseudo-Plutarch, was to deny this principle about opposites: one can have opposite potentialities at the same time.[35] Plato's new division of the soul is connected with a new appreciation, previously missing, that one sometimes wants what reason judges not to be best. Yet at the end of the *Republic*, Plato holds that outside this bodily life, the soul might still be best identified as the rational part that loves wisdom (*philosophia*),[36] although even on this there is subsequent wavering.[37]

That Aristotle thinks the human soul includes both rational and irrational elements we have seen. But it is rather surprising that he accepts Plato's argument from opposite desires as proving the point.[38] This is in spite of his apparently reinterpreting conflicts of desire as involving some kind of ignorance,[39] which should have avoided a head-on opposition between desires. It is also in spite of his apparently rejecting the idea that reason desires what it thinks best. Thinking is one thing, desiring another, and so reason should be distinguished from desire, and both categorised, not necessarily as distinct parts, but as distinct capacities.[40] It remains true that the capacity for reason and rational belief is only one of the capacities that constitutes the human soul.

The Stoics, however, under Chrysippus take a view even more intellectualist than that of the early Plato, who put into Socrates' mouth the view that one cannot want what one judges not to be best.[41] Chrysippus, according to some of the evidence, holds that wanting simply *is* a judgement of reason that it is appropriate (*kathēkei*) to act.[42] Similarly, emotions just *are* judgements of reason that there is good or bad in the offing and that it is appropriate to react accordingly.[43] Reason is now doing most of the work in the human soul. What Plato saw as a conflict of desire between reason and an irrational part of the soul is really just a matter of reason alone making conflicting judgements in rapid oscillation.

This intellectualism, in excess even of anything ascribed to Socrates, is too much for another good Stoic, Posidonius.[44] He says one will never understand emotions, if one forgets Plato's point that besides reason there is an emotional and irrational force in the soul, which tugs (*holkē*) at reason, as Plato had pointed out, when he compared the soul with a charioteer representing reason, and two horses.

Do animal souls include reason at all?

Reason may bulk more or less large in human souls, but is it found in animal souls at all?[45] Plato says different things, but sometimes allows, we saw, that an animal is a reincarnated human, equipped with a distorted and disused reason. Aristotle, by contrast denies reason to animals, and so has greatly to expand their perceptual powers to explain how they get around in the world. The Stoics also deny animals reason, but allow them to perceive, for example, that it is day. They further draw a moral conclusion. Their insistence that justice is owed to all humans, even to slaves and non-Greeks, was based on our common rationality. The downside of this benign, and historically influential, view was that no justice was owed to animals, since they lack reason. It was, unfortunately, this side of the ancient debate that Augustine took up and passed on to Christianity as the justification for killing animals. In fact there was an equally vigorous side to the ancient debate which claimed that animals were owed justice, and, since the Stoics had made this the criterion, did possess reason. The fullest case for this side, along with the opponents' arguments, is provided by the Neoplatonist Porphyry in one of the most interesting philosophical texts of antiquity, shortly to appear in a modern translation, *On Abstinence from Animal Food*.

Porphyry did not prevail with his fellow Neoplatonists, because they felt a religious obligation to perform animal sacrifice. But they were embarrassed at the thought that their grandmother's soul might be reincarnated within the sacrificial victim, as, on any unbiased reading, Plato had been willing to suppose. They therefore developed a theory that the distinctively human, rational soul would not enter inside the animal in reincarnation, but only direct the animal by a sort of remote control.

The case for animals having reason and being owed justice was belatedly recovered in the Renaissance, notably by Montaigne. Descartes had to overcome the influence of his fellow Frenchman. And in denying souls to animals altogether and making them automata, he went beyond anything in antiquity. At most, animals were denied by some of the ancients a rational part of the soul.

Part II: Self

Self not standardly soul

The self was not standardly equated in antiquity with soul. This was only one view among others, a view particularly connected with Plato.[46] In others we find much variety, with the concept of self sometimes including the body, sometimes only an aspect of the soul, and sometimes apparently something more abstract than either soul or body. There is also a large range of reasons for wanting to talk about the self, and no single word like 'self' for doing so.

The variety of concepts: self acting on self

This has implications for some of the extremely interesting and valuable literature on the self that has appeared in recent years, for it makes generalisation difficult. One view, taken in this volume by Galen Strawson, is that conceptions of the self are comparatively constant across cultures and that the central way in which we conceive of ourselves is as a mental thing, with the body as a distinct entity.[47] I believe it is a further presupposition that this self is conceived as being already there for inspection, rather than being constructed. In the last year an important study by Christopher Gill has offered an almost opposite view of the Greeks. They saw the self not only as embodied, but as participating in society.[48] I am not sure that any view can be right that looks for so much uniformity. I shall try to show that the self can be viewed in quite different ways even by the same author in the same context. And I believe this is perfectly natural because of the reflexive things that people want to say about the self. The self can be attached to the self, or conscious of the self (Hierocles), it can construct a self (Epictetus, cf. Plutarch), or direct a self, even directing it to another self (Plotinus). It is not always the same kind of self that is engaged at either end of these reflexive relations. Sometimes the self includes body, sometimes it is the soul, sometimes only a part or aspect of the soul, sometimes it may exclude soul as well as body. Sometimes it is constructed, sometimes already there for inspection, sometimes directed to society, sometimes not. Nor can one tell from the context what concept of self one will find. What I do agree with is the caveat which Galen Strawson enters, when he says, quite rightly, that our concept of self does not always include personality, nor the idea of continuity.

Recent literature has also included a large number of attacks sometimes on the whole idea of the self, sometimes on a particular philosophical idea of it. The very thin conceptions of self in Descartes, Locke and Kant have provoked the reaction either that there is no such thing,[49] or, in Kant's case, that it cannot do the work it is meant to in moral theory.[50] In this volume, Tony Kenny provides one example of a sophisticated attack on what he has elsewhere called the philosophical concept of the self as the product of a grammatical mistake. Descartes in his search for a self of which he could be certain, and Locke in his search for a self he could introspect, overlooked the fact that words like 'I' and 'myself' do not name anything. I am not clear that any of the ancient authors I shall be discussing was making a grammatical mistake, and I hope I am not doing so in interpreting them. Certainly, the range of philosophical concepts of the self and the range of motives for discussing selves is far greater than could be guessed from the cases of Descartes and Locke. It would not be possible, I believe, to maintain that these thinkers were all making the same mistake.

Biological and social contexts

Aristotle: the embodied person. In order to bring this out, I must give examples of the concepts of self deployed in ancient philosophy. This can be no more than the assembly of materials for further reflection and discussion. Aristotle writes in a biological context of the self as the embodied person. It would be as silly to say that the soul is angry, or pities, learns or thinks, as to say that it weaves or builds. It is the human (*anthrōpos*) who does so with his soul.[51]

Hierocles: the self's attachment to self. The Stoic Hierocles is one of those who has the self interact with the self. He does so in a combined biological and social context. It is natural for infants and new-born animals to feel an attachment (*oikeiōsis*) to themselves (*heauto*) and to their own constitution (*heautou sunthesis*), and to apprehend their body and soul which, it is said, is the same as apprehending themselves (*heautou*).[52] So far the object of attachment and perception is the embodied self. The moral conclusion is that we ought to extend this attachment to all humans in ever widening circles. When Hierocles makes this point, he imagines the individual (*hekastos*, *autos tis*) as surrounded by concentric circles, with other people further out, the circle that includes our body as 'almost the smallest', and the central circle as our mind (*dianoia*).[53] The individual that feels the attachment no longer includes the body, which is now part of the external surroundings. The individual may not even be the mind, for the mind is not said to be him, but his (*heautou*). Possibly then the individual self is seen as something very abstract, a sizeless point round which the mind forms the first circle and the body the next.[54] At any rate, the body is external to the self which feels attachment, even though it is included in the self to which attachment is felt.

Even though the context is one concerned with embodiment and participation in society, one of the two selves envisaged here is not embodied. In favour of the embodied participant conception Myles Burnyeat has been quoted for saying that ancient philosophy did not think of the body as part of the external world. But Burnyeat carefully confined his remark to epistemological contexts.[55] In fact the idea of one's body as external to oneself is quite common in Greek thought, starting from Plato's 'human within' (*anthrōpos entos*) in Book 9, which was very widely discussed.[56] Hierocles only provides a particularly vivid example.

Therapeutic contexts

Plutarch: The self weaving a biography.   I now pass from biological and social contexts to the therapeutic context of the search for tranquillity. The Platonist Plutarch seems to offer another reflexive example, this time of a self weaving a biography. He recommends in his treatise on tranquillity (*euthumia*) that we should weave our past into a biography with our present, instead of for ever dwelling on the future.[57] Otherwise we shall be like the man portrayed as weaving a rope in the house of Hades, who does not notice that a donkey is eating it up as fast as he weaves. We will then be like the momentary selves which are postulated by the so-called 'Growing argument', and which indeed Plutarch elsewhere speaks of as a reality. I shall come to these discontinuous selves below. Here they provide no more than a simile, and what Plutarch's weaving is said to create is not a single self, but a single life (*bion hena*). He is presupposing ordinary, continuous embodied selves, because the memories he wants us to weave into our biographies are genuine memories, that is memories of what we, the self-same persons, formerly did and experienced.

In Plutarch's example, besides the life which is woven, there is the self which does the weaving. The weaver is presumably the embodied self.

Daniel Dennett has used our ability to weave any number of biographies as evidence that the self is a fiction, albeit a convenient one. And he resists the idea that the self constructed presupposes a non-fictional self to do the constructing. The self just gets constructed through the interaction of separate systems in the brain which are no more unified than the ants in an anthill.[58] This is more radical than Plutarch. A closer analogy for Dennett's view is provided by the interpretation given to Homer by Bruno Snell, supported by Arthur Adkins.[59] Homer is said to give his heroes no unity or self, but to allow their decisions to remain the product of independent agencies within them. Modern scholarship has replied that selfhood (Dennett would say the fiction of selfhood) does not require more unity than Homer supplies.[60]

Epictetus: the self moulding an inviolable self.   There are other therapeutic views in which the self needs to construct not merely a life, but a self. The Stoic Epictetus offers a therapeutic concept of self designed to secure freedom from constraint. He had been a slave and had his leg broken. But the self he has constructed is something that cannot be violated. It is his *proairesis*, which might be translated 'will', although it is something more intellectual, the disposition of reason towards moral decisions. Epictetus imagines the following dialogue. 'I will fetter you.' 'What did you say, man? Fetter *me*? You will fetter my leg, but my will (*proairesis*) not even Zeus can conquer.'[61] The part about not being able to harm *me* was also ascribed to a much earlier thinker, Anaxarchus.[62] But the part about *proairesis* is Epictetus' own. This is by no means the only place where Epictetus implies he is not his body, but his *proairesis*.[63]

But the construction of such a self takes an effort. Epictetus says we can locate our self either in externals or in *proairesis*,[64] and our *proairesis* is something we can develop.[65] He describes the exercises he gives his students to produce this result.[66] They are to go out walking at dawn and ask themselves questions about the situations they encounter. They see a consul, or someone grieving over his child. They are to ask themselves if these things, office, death, or bereavement are subject to their will. If not, they are to apply the rule that nothing in the end matters that is not subject to the will. It may be rightly and naturally preferred or dispreferred. But what matters is simply their own character. The rest is, to use the Stoic word, indifferent.

What creates the inviolable self is evidently the embodied individual in society taking his walks in the city. But the self created is not only mental; it represents just one part of the mind, the *proairesis*. Moreover, I think there is a limit to the sense in which the inviolable self is a participant in society. Certainly, Epictetus points out many social duties which this self must recognise. But the Stoic doctrine of indifference means that what is important about these duties is the character they manifest. If, through no fault of the agent, just or generous actions do not succeed in relieving the needs of others, this is a matter of (dispreferred) indifference. The important thing is that good character has been exercised.[67]

Momentary selves. The idea, already encountered, that there are only short-lived, or momentary selves is by Plutarch and Seneca put to a certain therapeutic use. The idea itself is common. Plutarch refers not only as we have seen, to the Growing Argument, which will be further discussed below, but also cites Heraclitus, who says one cannot grasp mortal substance twice.[68] Plato both develops Heraclitus in the *Theaetetus* and explains love in the *Symposium* as a desire for offspring, to compensate us for our inability to stay the same like the gods.[69] I am not quite convinced by the ingenious suggestion that there is another example in Aristippus, who advocates concentrating on the pleasure of the present moment.[70] His rationale does not seem to be doubt whether there is a continuing self, but rather, in part, that memory and expectation cannot over a long time maintain the motion of the soul in which pleasure consists.[71] I think this presupposes a continuing self.

What is true is that some ancients used the kind of appeal to discontinuous selves that is a feature of Buddhism. Indeed, the Buddhist ideas feature in a dialogue, the *Questions of Milinda* between a Buddhist monk and a Greek Bactrian ruler, Menander, who is dated to the second century BC, although the original date of the work, which exists in Pali and Chinese, is disputed.[72] The intention of the argument is the therapeutic one of countering the fear of death, although the dialogue with the Buddhist draws further social conclusions about compassion for others. What Seneca and Plutarch both ask is: since our former selves have died many times, why do we fear a death will happen that has happened many times already?[73] Something closer to the full Buddhist treatment has been taken in contemporary philosophy by Derek Parfit.[74]

Seneca's use of this argument is not consistent with his elsewhere insisting that the constitution (*constitutio*) differs at different ages, but the self (*ego*, *me*) is always the same;[75] nor with his assuring Marcia that her son, because of his exceptional soul, will last until the next conflagration.[76] Plutarch could have argued consistently, if he had chosen, that the short-term selves should be woven together into a long-term biography. But in fact, we saw, when he recommends biographical weaving, he treats the short-term selves of the Growing Argument as no more than a simile. And in practice it would not have been possible to combine the therapy of weaving, to produce tranquillity, with the therapy of dwelling on discontinuity, to allay fear of death.

Dispersible and everlasting selves. There are other therapeutic concepts of self designed to allay different fears about death. The Epicureans drew comfort from the idea of a self dispersed at death, so exempt from subsequent punishment.[77] Plutarch complains that this overlooks the fear of annihilation.[78] Plato's Socrates had offered the opposite solace, more familiar to the Christian tradition, of an everlasting self.[79]

19

RICHARD SORABJI

Eudaimonistic and soteriological contexts

The contemplative self in Plato and Aristotle. Although Plato identifies soul and self, *Republic* Book 10 suggests that the true soul and the true self may be only that part of the soul which loves wisdom (*philosophia*) in other words, the rational part.[80] And there is plenty of other evidence that, for Plato, it is the rational soul, or part of the soul, that is the true self. This in the *Timaeus,* though not in the *Phaedrus*, is the only immortal part of the soul.[81]

Aristotle also says that each person (*hekastos*) is thought to be his intellect (*nous*), or reason (*dianoētikon*). When he first says this, he is thinking particularly of practical reason,[82] but he repeats it in a context which focuses on the contemplative reason that understands science and metaphysics.[83] He considers what kind of life would be led by the gods, or by those, if there are any, who are fabled to go after death to the Isles of the Blessed. They would have neither money, nor dangers to face, so most of the conventional virtues would be irrelevant. What is left is the contemplation of truth. So that would be the happiest life for humans too.[84] Aristotle confronts the objection, however, that that would be a divine, not a human, life. And that is his occasion for replying that each person is thought to be his intellect.

Directing the self to the contemplative self. Plotinus also sees the life of intellectual contemplation as the happiest.[85] He distinguishes three powers in the soul, which he sometimes calls three selves (*hēmeis*). Below there is that concerned with the body involving perception and emotion. Above there is the soul which is uninterruptedly contemplating the world of Forms, even though we are normally unconscious of it. But the true person (*alēthēs anthrōpos*), that which he sometimes singles out for calling us (*hēmeis*), is the intermediate power of step-by-step reasoning which Plotinus calls, after Plato *Republic* Book 9, the human within.[86] This is the true person not in the sense of the best, since there is a better self. But it is pivotal. For Plotinus further says that our intermediate self can be directed upwards towards the activity of contemplating, or downwards towards bodily activities.[87] Indeed, it can be directed by us (*taxōmen*: is this the embodied self as a whole?).[88] We can act in accordance with any of the three selves, and each individual (*hekastos*) actually is the one in accordance with whom he acts.[89] This means that our reasoning self can actually come to be the self that uninterruptedly contemplates.

20

Plotinus is very conscious of worries about our maintaining our identities. He repeatedly discusses how there is a sense in which all our higher selves, our contemplative souls, are one, and yet how they are also distinct.[90] The subject is further discussed by Porphyry and Augustine.[91] Plotinus is also very conscious that in mystical union with higher entities, the Intellect or the One, we lose all sense of our own boundaries.[92]

The contemplative self and personality. Galen Strawson's question whether the self includes personality is very pressing in connection with the contemplative self. This remains so, even though Plato insists on reason having many desires and pleasures of its own,[93] and Aristotle and Plotinus are keenly aware of the joys of contemplation. The threat to personality is vividly brought out by the view held by certain sixth-century Origenists and ascribed, erroneously, to their forebear Origen, that our resurrection bodies will be completely spherical.[94] Chrysippus the Stoic thinks our souls are themselves material and will be after death spherical.[95] Among the Neoplatonists, Iamblichus thinks our souls are housed in spherical vehicles of tenuous matter.[96] And Plotinus considers the implications for personality, if souls after death have only spherical vehicles. It is striking that even in this soteriological context, we are not thought of as altogether disembodied. Plotinus envisages that our souls may have got rid of emotions. But he thinks of them retaining memory and character (*ēthē*), and supposes that, despite the spherical vehicles, the individuality of their behaviour (*idiotēs tōn tropōn*) might persist, and that they might recognise each other through that. This would be all the easier if they could talk.[97]

None of this however, concerns those souls which travel still higher to contemplation in the intelligible world. They will neither remember their past nor display character, at least until they start returning for reincarnation.[98]

Augustine also feels some tension between the contemplative ideal and his intense personal relationships. In the *Confessions*, he wonders if his momentary experience of mystical contact with God might be what the saints enjoy uninterruptedly.[99] He describes the life of those in the heaven of heavens as one of rapt contemplation of God, in which there is no awareness of past, present or future.[100] Consequently, there is no time, given his theory that time consists of such awareness.[101] Yet in another part of the *Confessions* he hopes that his dead friend will not be too drunk with the fountain of wisdom to remember him.[102] And although he rejects the value of genetic relationships in the kingdom of God,[103] and thinks of his parents in that connection rather as brethren and fellow citizens,[104] it has been pointed out that he does so almost in the same breath as his affectionate description of his beloved mother's last days and of their shared mystical experience.[105]

Although this can only be a preliminary sketch, its aim is to show the enormous variety of concepts of the self in ancient philosophy, and of contexts for discussing the self. Moreover, contexts and concepts have turned out to vary independently of each other. I believe this variety defies any attempt to find a single dominant conception, or a single mistake that makes all the conceptions chimerical. But despite a good number of modern parallels, some of the conceptions of the self I have been stressing may seem remote from modern philosophical concerns. So one thing remains to be done. That is to show that ancient philosophy was no less engrossed with other questions about the self that are central today.

Personal identity over time

Many modern philosophical discussions have concentrated on two questions. What makes a person the same person over a period of time? And what makes one person distinct from another? In fact ancient philosophy initiated some of the puzzles that are still being discussed in today's philosophical journals.

Endless recurrence and distinguishability. To take identity over time, many Stoics and some Pythagoreans thought history would exactly repeat itself an infinite number of times. The persons would be the same as before, because there would be nothing to distinguish them, except the time. The times would allegedly be different, even though there was nothing to distinguish them either. I have discussed this theme and variations on it elsewhere.[106] The Aristotelian Eudemus objected that the time would be the same, given Aristotle's definition of time as the countable aspect of change, since every countable aspect would be the same.[107] The theory of recurrence led to a debate on whether, in order to be us, it would be necessary or sufficient for the later people to be indistinguishable from us.

Some Stoics held that even if the population in the next cycle of the universe were indistinguishable (*aparallaktos*) from the present population and in indistinguishable circumstances, they would not be the same people.[108] Others asked if the difference of temporal location (*katataxis*) would mean there were different me's, that is, several of the same person.[109] Others thought the people could be the same, even if they had inessential differences, like freckles.[110]

Alexander took the view that after an interruption we would not have numerically the same Socrates, even if the same matter was reassembled. For the interruption would prevent it being the same individual form (*atomon eidos*).[111] We will see Philoponus saying something similar in his treatment of growth.[112]

Persistence through growth and difference of matter. Equally within a single life time, the Stoics discussed what makes a person the same person throughout a whole life. Drawing on Plato's *Theaetetus*,[113] they postulated the continuation of a uniquely distinctive bundle of qualities throughout the whole of one's life.[114] Later, the view was attributed, I think wrongly, to the Aristotelian school and apparently favoured by Porphyry that individuals are nothing but a bundle of such qualities.[115] In fact Aristotle had only explored distinctive characteristics for individuals rather tentatively when dealing in his biological works with inherited characteristics.[116]

This was evidently one of many answers to puzzles about how a living individual can persist, given that in the process of growth its matter is always being replaced, and sometimes also changing in quantity. These puzzles appear early in the fifth century BC in the comic playwright Epicharmus.[117] Some of them are given the name of the 'Growing Argument'.[118] Answers alternative to the Stoics' persistence of unique qualities are the Aristotelian answer that form persists, the answer that soul persists, that although we do not have the same primary matter, we have the same secondary subject, e.g. bronze or Socrates, that there is the same indivisible but composite essence involving some type of matter and form.[119] It is argued on behalf of Aristotle that form can persist, provided the replacement of matter occurs bit by bit, not all in one go.[120]

The ship of Theseus and difference of matter. The problem, it was pointed out, is not quite the same as that of the inanimate statue or ship, the ship of Theseus, which is thought to persist, even when all of its parts have been replaced.[121] Solutions to the growth problem assume that identity over time does not require the same matter to persist. But Philoponus comments that there is an independent reason to think that some of an animal's matter needs to persist. For if it could all be safely replaced, we should be immortal.[122]

Resurrection and sameness of matter. Sameness of matter over time
was also required for the puzzle about bodily resurrection found in
Tatian, Tertullian, ps.-Athenagoras, Origen and Porphyry, and subsequently discussed by both Augustine and Thomas Aquinas.[123] If a
cannibal eats me, or if my flesh passes via carnivorous beasts into carnivorous humans, will there be enough matter left for us both to be
resurrected? For Origen, this was part of a series of arguments
designed to show that our resurrection bodies will not contain the
same matter. Human flesh and blood cannot be reconstituted as such,
any more than wine thrown into the sea.[124] What is passed on to the
resurrection body is only an improved form (*eidos*) of the earlier
body.[125] But for those who believed the same matter would be
needed, the problem was serious, even though for some of them, no
bodily requirements need be met for sameness of our rational soul,
and hence of ourselves. For there will be a stage in Purgatory before
any resurrection, when our will is disembodied and punished for past
sins.[126] This intermediate separation of soul is also found in early
Church Fathers,[127] although for Tertullian the soul is a body.[128]

Chance reassembly and sameness of matter. The question arose not only
whether sameness of matter was necessary, but whether it was sufficient for the survival of ourselves (*nos*). This was denied not only
by Alexander commenting on the Stoics' recurring universe, but
also by the Epicurean atomist, Lucretius. On his view, the atoms
that now compose our bodies might by chance reassemble in the
same order as now, long after our deaths, in the infinity of time.
Like John Locke after him, Lucretius comments that would be of
no use to us (*nec pertinere*), if the memory of our past life was interrupted (*interrupta*). Nonetheless, he does concede that the atoms
reassembled in the right order would be us.[129] It is not clear whether
Epicurean materialism implies that the identically reassembled
person remembers his past life after an interruption,[130] or does not
remember it at all.

Forms of individuals. Plotinus considers whether there is a Platonic
Form (*idea*) for each individual person.[131] He compares the Stoic
view that each person within a cycle of world history has a distinct
forming principle (*logos*), though the same *logos* in the next cycle.[132]
Plotinus may or may not eventually reject the view. One difficulty
he considers is reincarnation. Suppose Socrates was formerly one
soul, but can be reincarnated as a different soul, say, Pythagoras.
Would there then be a Form of Socrates? There could hardly be the

same *logos* for different individuals.[133] This difficulty ought to lead on to a further doubt. If reincarnation involves one individual being reincarnated as another, does it provide for the survival of a self in a way that can at all assuage the fear of annihilation? The Forms about which Plotinus is inquiring cannot bestow identity on Socrates. No one had comparable difficulty with the idea they ascribe to Aristotle that each individual has a distinct Aristotelian form (*eidos*), whose identity is, however, partly derivative from that of the individual.[134]

Differentiation of individuals

Ancient philosophy was equally concerned with the modern problem of what differentiates individuals, and I shall finish with one striking problem that arises in Stoicism, and which has been the subject of a masterly exposition by David Sedley although it may still be worth seeing if another interpretation can be found.[135]

The Stoics held that individuals were differentiated by having those uniquely distinguishing bundles of qualities which also supply continuing identity[136] and Porphyry and Boethius seem to have agreed.[137] But this is cited by later sources as only one among several rival answers. Another answer is that individuals need to be spatially separated.[138] Other answers include matter and material circumstances,[139] or form.[140]

The Stoics did not insist on spatial separation at least for materials in chemical combination. They allowed that water and wine, for example, could be mixed into exactly the same place as each other. In the mixture, the distinctive qualities of each are preserved and can 'show forth together'. Moreover, the distinct matters may be preserved, if *ousia* in this context means matter. Later the original ingredients can be re-separated and the Stoics may think of this as the retrieval of the very same water and wine.[141] Some of this may be relevant to the Stoic puzzle of Dion and Theon, two people who, on Sedley's interpretation, overlap in the same place. Only two things are forbidden by the Stoic Chrysippus. Two individuals cannot occupy exactly the same substance or substrate, in other words the same matter. And they must not lose their unique qualities. This combines qualities with matter as a condition of difference.

In his treatise *On the Growing (Argument)* the Stoic Chrysippus imagines two men, one with two feet and one with only one, who, on Sedley's interpretation, are in the same place as each other, except that one foot does not overlap. Chrysippus makes the startling claim that if the foot of the whole-limbed man is now amputated, one of the two men will perish. And this is against the background of the claim that two individuals with uniquely differentiating characteristics cannot occupy the same substance.[142] What is going on? A solution needs to do several things. One is to explain why Chrysippus does not blow the whistle earlier: why he raises no objection to Theon *partly* overlapping with Dion. Another is to say what positive motive there could be for anyone to suppose that Theon does exist within Dion.

The later medieval version of the problem in William of Sherwood bears on this pair of issues, but does not immediately reveal how the original puzzle went. It focuses on the question whether Socrates minus his foot is, before the amputation, a person, or merely part of a person.[143] For now, I shall leave the reconstruction of the original puzzle as a puzzle.[144]

Notes

1 Descartes, reply to objections brought against the 2nd Meditation, para. 4, in the *5th Objections*, trans. Haldane and Ross, vol. 2, p. 210, on which see Richard Sorabji, 'Body and Soul in Aristotle', *Philosophy* 49 (1974), 63–89, at p. 65, repr. in Barnes, Schofield, and B. Sorabji *Articles on Aristotle*, 4 (1979), 42–64, at 44.
2 Aristotle *On the Soul* 2.1–4, and further references in Sorabji, op. cit.
3 Plato *Timaeus* 77 a–b; Empedocles frag. 117, Diels–Kranz; Friedrich Solmsen, 'Antecedents of Aristotle's psychology and scale of beings', *American Journal of Philology* 76 (1955), 148–64.
4 Aristotle *On the Soul* 2.4, 416a15–18.
5 Ibid. 3.3, 428a19–24; b3–4; Richard Sorabji, *Animal Minds and Human Morals* (London and Ithaca, NY, 1993), chs 1, 2.
6 Aristotle *Nic.Eth.* 3.10, 1118a20–3.
7 Aristotle *History of Animals* 8.1, 588b4–23; *Parts of Animals* 4.5, 681a10–18. For Aristotle's futher doubts, see G.E.R. Lloyd 'Fuzzy natures' in his *Aristotelian Explorations* (Cambridge, 1996). Andrew Coles, 'Animal and childhood cognition in Aristotle's biology and the scala naturae', in W. Kullmann and S. Föllinger, (eds.), *Aristotelische Biologie* (Stuttgart, 1997), 287–323.
8 References in Sorabji, *Animal Minds and Human Morals*, ch. 8, esp. 98–9.
9 Aristotle *On the Soul* 2.4, 415b8–28.
10 Richard Sorabji, *Necessity, Cause and Blame* (London and Ithaca, NY, 1980), ch. 10.
11 John Burnet, 'The Socratic doctrine of the soul', *Proceedings of the British Academy* 1915–16, 235–59.
12 Homer *Odyssey* 11.

SOUL AND SELF IN ANCIENT PHILOSOPHY

13 R. B. Onians, *The Origins of European Thought* (Cambridge, 1951; 2nd edn 1954), Part I.
14 Plato *Phaedo* 86c.
15 Nemesius *On the Nature of Man* 2.17.5–9, p. 537 M; cf. Aëtius *Placita* 4.2.5 in H. Diels *Doxographici Graeci* (1879).
16 Galen *Quod animi mores* 44.12–20.
17 Ibid. 36.12–16.
18 Andronicus in Galen *Quod animi mores* 44.12–20; Alexander *On the soul* 24.1–5; 24.18–25.9; 26.7–30; Alexander(?) *Mantissa* (= *de Intellectu*) 112.14–16; Philoponus *in DA* 191.11–25; 439.35–440.3. On the soul's perceptual capacity, see Victor Caston, 'Epiphenomenalisms ancient and modern', *Philosophical Review* (1997) who points out that Dicaearchus' equation of soul with bodily blend was wrongly called a denial of soul.
19 H. von Arnim, *Stoicorum Veterorum Fragmenta (SVF)* (1903–) 2.809–11.
20 P. Hadot, 'The harmony of Plotinus and Aristotle according to Porphyry', translated from the French of 1974, and Richard Sorabji, 'The ancient commentators on Aristotle', both in Richard Sorabji (ed.), *Aristotle Transformed: The Ancient Commentators and their Influence* (London and Ithaca, N.Y, 1990).
21 See esp. *Odyssey* Book 11 and lines 204–24.
22 Plato *Phaedo* 78b–84b.
23 Plato *Timaeus* 36c–37A; 38c–40a; 41d–42a; 43a–44d; 67a–b; 91e–92a; *Laws* 790d–791b. The point has been made orally by David Sedley.
24 Plato *Phaedo* 81c–d.
25 e.g. Philoponus *in DA* 17.19–18.33.
26 Epicurus *Letter to Herodotus* 67; Lucretius 1.418–48; 3.161–7; Cleanthes in Nemesius *On the Nature of Man* p. 32 M (*SVF* 1.518); Plutarch *Comm.Not.* 1073E (*SVF* 2.525); 1080F; Diogenes Laertius *Lives* 7.55 (*SVF* 2.140); Sextus *M* 8.263 (*SVF* 2.363); Sextus *PH* 3.38; Seneca *Ep.* 106.2 (*SVF* 3.84); Cicero *Ac.Pr.* 11.39 (*SVF* 1.90); Aëtius *Placita* 4.20.2 in *Dox.Gr.* 410.6 (*SVF* 2.387); ps.–Galen *Hist.Phil.* ch. 23 'On bodies', *Dox.Gr.* 612.19–613.2.
27 Epicurus *Letter to Herodotus* in Diogenes Laertius *Lives* 63, 66; Lucretius 3.94–416.
28 *SVF* 2.773–787.
29 G. Verbeke, *L' Évolution de la doctrine du pneuma du Stoicisme à S. Augustin* (Paris, 1945).
30 Aristotle *On the Soul* 1.3, 407a2–3.
31 Ibid. 1.3, 407b20–6.
32 Augustine *On the Trinity* 10.10.14–16.
33 The findings of E. L. Fortin and H. Dörrie are summarised by Gerard O'Daly, *Augustine's Philosophy of Mind*, London 1987. They refer to Porphyry *ap.* Nemesium *On the Nature of Man*; ch. 3, paras. 3–5, pp. 127–9M; Priscian *Solutiones*, *CAG* supp. vol. 1, p. 51, line 4 ff.; Augustine *Ep.* 137,11. The sponge experiment was successfully performed in my presence in 1985 by Connie Meinwald and Wolfgang Mann. The Stoic theory is discussed in Richard Sorabji (ed.), *Matter, Space and Motion* (London and Ithaca, NY, 1988), ch. 6.
34 Plato *Republic* 436b–440b.
35 ps.–Plutarch, Tyrwhitt frag. 2, ch. 2. in Loeb Plutarch xv, 62.

27

36 Plato *Republic* 611b–612a.
37 Plato *Phaedrus* 246a ff.
38 Aristotle *Nic.Eth.* 1.13, 1102b13–31.
39 Ibid. 7.3, on the usual interpretation.
40 Aristotle *On the Soul* 3.9, 432a 22–31, on the usual interpretation.
41 See e.g. Plato *Protagoras* 358b–e; *Gorgias* 468 b–d; *Meno* 77e–78b.
42 Stobaeus 2.88.1 with 2.86.17–18.
43 Cicero *Tusc.* 4.14; Diogenes Laertius *Lives* 7.111; Galen *PHP* 4.2.5–6; 4.3.1–2; 5.1.4. Richard Sorabji, 'Is Stoic philosophy helpful as psychotherapy?, in his (ed.), *Aristotle and After, Bulletin of the Institute of Classical Studies*, supplement 68 (1997), 197–209, and in *Emotion and Peace of Mind: from Stoic Agitation to Christian Temptation*, Oxford, forthcoming.
44 Galen *PHP* 4–5; Sorabji *Emotions*, forthcoming.
45 References for this section are supplied in Sorabji, *Animal Minds and Human Morals*.
46 Plato *Phaedo* 63b–c; 115C; *Republic* 469 d6–9; cf. *Protagoras* 313a–b; and, if it is by Plato, *First Alcibiades* 130a.
47 Galen Strawson, 'The sense of self', *London Review of Books*, 18 April 1996, 21–2, and this volume.
48 Christopher Gill, 'The human being as ethical norm' in his (ed.) *The Person and the Human Mind* (Oxford 1990); *Personality in Greek Epic, Tragedy, and Philosophy*, (Oxford, 1996), *passim*.
49 See David Hume *A Treatise of Human Nature* (252 in L.A. Selby-Bigge, Oxford, 1888, reprinted 1958); Wittgenstein *Philosophical Investigations* (Oxford, 1953), 413 on William James; Elizabeth Anscombe, 'The first person', in S. Guttenplan (ed.), *Mind and Language* (Oxford 1975), repr. in her *Collected Philosophical Papers*, ii (Cambridge, 1991); Derek Parfit *Reasons and Persons* (Oxford, 1984); A. Kenny, 'The self', *The Aquinas Lecture*, (Marquette University, Wis., 1988–9), and in this volume; Daniel Dennett, 'Why everyone is a novelist', *Times Literary Supplement* 16–22 Sept. 1988, 1016, 1028–9; *Consciousness Explained*, (Boston, 1991).
50 Bernard Williams *Ethics and the Limits of Philosophy* (London, 1985); Alasdair MacIntyre *After Virtue* (London, 1985).
51 Aristotle *On the soul* 1.4, 408b11–15.
52 Hierocles *Elementa Moralia* 6.49–53; 4.51–3, ed. A. A. Long, *Corpus dei papiri filosofici greci e latini* (Florence, 1992).
53 Hierocles in Stobaeus *Florilegium*, Heinze and Wachsmuth, iv 671, lines 7 ff.
54 For a very abstract concept in modern literature, cf. Thomas Nagel, *The View from Nowhere* (New York 1986), ch. 4.
55 Myles Burnyeat, 'Idealism and Greek Philosophy; What Descartes saw and Berkeley missed', *Philosophical Review* 91 (1982), 3–40, cited by Gill, *Personality,* 409–10. Cf. Charles Taylor, *Sources of the Self* (1989), 121.
56 See e.g. Theo Heckel *Der innere Mensch* (Tübingen, 1993), on the man within in Plato *Republic* 588b–589b, and its influence on St Paul, Philo and the Nag Hammadi Gnostics, to which add Plotinus 1.1.10(15); 1.1.7(20)
57 Plutarch *On Tranquillity* 473B–474B.

58 Daniel Dennett, op. cit. n. 49.
59 Bruno Snell, *Die Entdeckung des Geistes*, trans. as *The Discovery of the Mind* (New York, 1960), chs 1 and 5; Arthur Adkins *From the Many to the One* (London, 1970).
60 For various replies, see R. W. Sharples, '"But why has my spirit spoken within me thus?" Homeric decision-making', *Greece and Rome* 30 (1983), 1–7; Richard Gaskin, 'Do Homeric heroes make real decisions?', *Classical Quarterly* 40 (1990), 1–15; Bernard Williams *Shame and Necessity* (Berkeley, 1993), ch. 2; discussion in Gill, *Personality,* ch. 1.
61 Epictetus *Discourses* 1.1.23; cf. 4.1.72–80; *Handbook* 9.
62 Philo *Every virtuous person is free,* ch. 17,109; Gregory of Nazianzus *Ep.* 32.
63 See e.g. 3.1.40; *Handbook* 18.
64 Epictetus 2.2.19–20; 2.2.28.
65 Epictetus 1.4.18; 3.5.7.
66 Epictetus 3.3.14–19; cf. 3.8.1–5.
67 I have discussed this aspect of Stoicism in *Animal Minds and Human Morals*, chs 10–11.
68 Plutarch *On the E at Delphi* 392b–c = Heraclitus frag. 91, Diels-Kranz.
69 Plato *Symposium* 207d4–208a3; *Theaetetus* 152c–153d; 181b–183c.
70 Terence Irwin, 'Aristippus against happiness', *The Monist* 74 (1991), 55–82.
71 Diogenes Laertius *Lives* 2.89–90.
72 There is a French translation from the Pali of 1923, and a German translation of 1985.
73 Seneca *Letters* 24.19–21, 58.22–3; Plutarch *On the E at Delphi* 392c–e.
74 Derek Parfit, *Reasons and Persons* (Oxford, 1984); Steven Collins, *Selfless Persons* (Cambridge, 1982).
75 Seneca *Letters* 121.16.
76 Seneca *On Consolation to Marcia* 26.6–7.
77 Epicurus *Kuriai Doxai* 2; Lucretius 3. 31–93, 830–1094.
78 Plutarch, *That Epicurus makes a pleasant life impossible* 1104a–1105c.
79 Plato *Phaedo.*
80 In *Phaedo* 63b-c; 115c it is only the rational soul that Plato is considering. In *Republic* 588b–589b the inner man, representing reason, seems to be the true self. See also Sarah Waterlow (later Broadie) 'The good of others in Plato's Republic', *Proceedings of the Aristotelian Society* 73 (1972–3), 19–36.
81 Plato *Timaeus* 69c.
82 Aristotle *Nic.Eth.* 9.4, 1166a17; 9.8, 1168b34–1169a2.
83 *Nic.Eth.* 10.7, 1178a2.
84 Aristotle *Protrepticus* frag. 12, Ross, Walzer; *Nic.Eth.* 10.8, 1178b8–23; imitated by Cicero in his lost *Hortensius*, quoted by Augustine *On the Trinity* 14.9.12, who comments that justice would still be needed.
85 Plotinus 1.5.7.
86 1.1.7(17–24); 1.1.10; 5.3.3(34–9).
87 1.1.11(1–8); 2.9.2(4–18).
88 1.1.11(7).
89 6.7.6(15–18); cf 6.4.15(37).
90 Plotinus 4.9.1–5; 4.2; 4.3.1–8; 6.4.4 and 14–15; 6.5.12.
91 Porphyry *Sentences* 37 (commenting on Plotinus 6.4); and *ap.* Nemesium *On the Nature of Man* 2, p. 110, 8–10 M (discussing Manicheans);

p. 112, 8–9 M; Augustine *de Quantitate Animae* 69. This is different from the question whether Aristotle's agent intellect is the same for all humans, on which Thomas Aquinas considered as a crucial text Themistius *in DA* 103, 32–8

92 References in Sorabji, *Time, Creation and the Continuum*, 159, nn. 20 to 30, 160 nn. 41 to 47.

93 Plato e.g. *Phaedo* 114e; *Republic* 439b–442d; 581c–588a.

94 Origen in Justinian *Ep. ad Mennam*, Mansi 9, 516D; cf. anathema 10 of the Second Council of Constantinople. For correction, see Henry Chadwick, 'Origen, Celsus and the resurrection of the body', *Harvard Theological Review* 41 (1948), 83–102.

95 *SVF* 2.815.

96 Iamblichus *ap.* Proclum *in Tim.* 2.72.14.

97 4.4.5(12–31).

98 4.4.5(23–27); 4.3.32; 4.4.1.

99 Augustine *Confessions* 9.10.

100 Ibid. Books 12–13.

101 Ibid. Book 11.

102 Ibid. 9.3.

103 *On the True Religion* 46.88–8.

104 *Confessions* 9.13.

105 Ibid. 9.10. This and many other of the points in this paragraph are made by R. J. O'Connell, *St. Augustine's Confessions: an Odyssey of Soul* (Cambridge, Mass, 1969); discussion in Sorabji, *Time, Creation and the Continuum*, ch. 11.

106 Sorabji, *Matter, Space and Motion,* ch. 10, esp. 163–4; 180–1, with literature cited there; *Time, Creation and the Continuum* 182–190.

107 Simplicius *in Phys.* 732.26–733.1.

108 Origen *contra Celsum* 4.68 (*SVF* 2.626).

109 Simplicius *in Phys.* 886.11 (*SVF* 2.627).

110 Alexander *in An.Pr.* 181.25 (*SVF* 2.624); Origen *contra Celsum* 5.20 (*SVF* 2.626).

111 Alexander *ap.* Philoponum *in GC* 314.9–22.

112 Philoponus *in GC* 106.3–11.

113 Plato *Theaetetus* 209a-d, 157b-c; Sorals: *Matter, Space and Motion* ch. 4.

114 Posidonius frag. 96 Edelstein Kidd, from Arius Didymus in Stobaeus 1.178, 13–21, Wachsmuth; 'Simplicius' *in DA* 217.36 ff (*SVF* 2.395); Simplicius *in Cat* 140.24–30; P. Oxy. 3008 in P. Parsons, (ed.), *Ox.Pap.* XLII, 30–1.

115 Porphyry *Isagoge* 7.19–27; Proclus *ap.* Olympiodorum *in Alcibiades* (Creuzer) 204; Philoponus *in An.Post.* 437,21–438,2.

116 D. M. Balme, 'Aristotle's biology was not essentialist', *Archiv für Geschichte der Philosophie* 62 (1980), 1–12; R.W. Sharples, 'Species, form and inheritance: Aristotle and after', in Allan Gotthelf (ed.), *Aristotle on Nature and Living Things* (Pittsburgh and Bristol, 1985).

117 See the reconstruction by David Sedley, 'The Stoic criterion of identity', *Phronesis* 27 (1982), 255–75 at 255.

118 Plutarch *Comm.Not.* 1083B–C; and references in next note. There are roots of the puzzle in the insistence on flux in Heraclitus, famously in frag. 91 Diels–Kranz from Plutarch *On the E* 392 B–C, in his

follower Cratylus and in Plato's development of Heraclitus at *Theaetetus* 152c–153d; 181b–183c.

119 Aristotle *GC* 1.5; Philoponus *in GC* 102.31–111.13; Simplicius *in Cat.* 140.25–31; Ghazali in Averroes *Destruction of the Destruction* ed. Bouyges 571, trans. van den Bergh 353–4. For secondary subject, see Porphyry in Simplicius *in Cat.* 48.13–16; Philoponus *in Phys.* 579.3–5; *Contra Proclum* 426.22–3.

120 Philoponus *in GC* 106.3–11.

121 Ibid. 106.18–23; Plutarch *Life of Theseus* 23.

122 Philoponus *in GC* 107.3–7.

123 Tatian *Oratio ad Gr.* 6; Tertullian *de Resurrectione*, 30 Kroymann; Origen *Comm. on Psalm 1* in Methodius *de Resurrectione* 1.20.4–5, GCS 27 = Epiphanius *Panarion* 64.12.6–8; Porphyry *Against the Christians* frag. 94 Harnack from Macarius Magnes 4.24, TU 37.4 (Leipzig 1911), 92; Augustine *City of God* 22.12 and 20; (ps?)-Athenagoras *de Resurrectione* 5–7.1; Thomas Aquinas *Summa Theologiae* 3 supplement, q.80, a.4. See Henry Chadwick, 'Origen, Celsus and the resurrection of the body', *Harvard Theological Review* 41, (1948), 83–102; R. M. Grant, 'Athenagoras or pseudo-Athenagoras?', *Harvard Theological Review* 49 (1956), 115–129 at 124–5; M. J. Edwards, 'Origen's two resurrections', *Journal of Theological Studies* 46 (1995), 502–18 at 517–18.

124 Origen in Methodius *de Resurrectione* 1.14–15; Jerome *adv. Joh. Hier. ad Pamm.* 25 M.P.L. 23, 376 BC

125 Methodius *de Resurrectione* 1.25.2; 1.22.3–5, GCS 27.

126 Thomas Aquinas *Summa Theologiae*, 3 supplement q.70, a.3, and appendix: question on purgatory.

127 Tertullian *On the Soul*, ch. 55.3; ch. 58.8.

128 Ibid., chs 5–8.

129 Lucretius 3. 847–51. Cicero is less clear, calling our Epicurean duplicates innumerable, *Ac.* 2.125. Does this make them distinct from us?

130 Thanks to Verity Harte for this doubt, based on David Sedley, 'Epicurean anti-reductionism', in Jonathan Barnes and Mario Mignucci (eds.), *Matter and Metaphysics*, (Bibliopolis, 1988).

131 Plotinus 5.7.1–3; 5.9.12; 6.5.8. See H. J. Blumenthal, *Plotinus' Psychology* (the Hague, 1971), ch. 9, 'Ideas of individuals'; A. H. Armstrong, 'Form, individual and person in Plotinus', *Dionysius* 1 (1977), 49–68, repr. in his *Plotinian and Christian Studies* (Variorum, 1979); John Rist, 'Ideas of individuals in Plotinus, a reply to Dr. Blumenthal', *Revue internationale de philosophie* 24 (1970), 298–303.

132 5.7.2(22–3).

133 5.7.1(3–10; 19–22).

134 A.C. Lloyd, *Form and Universal in Aristotle* (Liverpool, 1981).

135 David Sedley, 'The Stoic criterion of identity', *Phronesis* 27 (1982), 255–75.

136 See Plutarch *Comm.Not.* 1077C.

137 Porphyry *in Cat.* 129.8–10; *Isagoge* 7.21–7; Boethius *in Isag.* 2, ed. Brandt, 235.5–236.6; *in Int.* 2, ed. Meiser, 136.17–137.26. Boethius' coining of the word *Platonitas*, however, could well invite misunderstanding

138 Dexippus *in Cat.* 30.20–4; Simplicius *in Cat.* 229,17–8; Boethius *On the Trinity* 1, lines 24–31.
139 Alexander *Quaestio* 1.3, 7.27–8.6; *DA* 85.15–20; 90.2–11.
140 For Plotinus on Forms of individuals, see above.
141 Alexander *On Mixture* 216.32–217.2; Arius Didymus frag. 28, *Dox.Gr.* 464.1–6, trans with discussion in Sorabji, *Matter, Space and Motion*, 80–3.
142 Philo *On the eternity of the world* 48 (*SVF* 2.397).
143 William of Sherwood, *Treatise on Syncategorematic Words;* ch. 10, para. 6 '*Praeter*', trans. Norman Kretzmann (Minneapolis, 1968). I thank him for the reference.
144 The opportunity to write about the Self for this volume has provided the subject for my next book (after the forthcoming one on Emotions cited above – see Note 43.)

3

BODY, SOUL, AND INTELLECT IN AQUINAS

Anthony Kenny

St Thomas Aquinas, who in the twentieth century has been considered an official spokesman for Roman Catholic orthodoxy, was in his own day an adventurous philosopher whose teaching was regarded by many theologians with suspicion. Just three years after his death the congregation of Oxford University, following the lead of colleagues in Paris, condemned, without naming him, a number of propositions which he had maintained. Those who taught these Thomist theses were to be allowed forty days to recant; if they continued to hold them they were to lose their MAs.

The part of Aquinas' teaching which got him into trouble at Oxford was his application of the Aristotelian theory of form and matter to the nature of the human soul. For Aristotle material substances like a bit of wood consisted of matter possessing certain forms. A piece of wood possesses accidental forms, such as its shape, colour, and temperature which can be varied while it remains wood; it also possesses a substantial form which makes it the kind of thing it is, namely wood. If it is burnt and turns into ash so that it ceases to be wood, then the same matter which once existed with the substantial form of wood now exists with the substantial form of ash. The very same parcel of matter was once wood and is now ash. What was it all the time? Nothing, said Aquinas; all that remains in common is identity of matter – prime matter, in the technical expression, namely matter considered in abstraction from any particular form it may take as one or other particular kind of matter.

Following Aristotle, Aquinas used the doctrine of matter and form as the key to the relationship between soul and body. For Aristotle animals and vegetables had souls no less then human beings. The vegetative, or nutritive, soul was the explanatory principle of the growth and propagation of plants; the sensitive soul was the explanatory principle of the sensory activities of animals. What made human beings special was not simply the possession of a soul, but the possession of a rational or intellectual soul. Now human beings grow and take nourishment, just as plants do; they see and taste and run and sleep just as animals do. Does that mean that they have a vegetable and animal soul as well as a human soul?

Many of St Thomas' contemporaries answered in the affirmative. In a human being, they maintained, there was not just a single form, the intellectual soul, but also sensitive and nutritive souls governing the animal and vegetable functions of the human being. Some theorists added, for good measure, a form which made a human being a bodily being, namely a form of corporality, which humans had in common with sticks and stones just as they had sensitive souls in common with animals and vegetative souls in common with plants.

St Thomas rejected the proliferation of substantial forms. In a human being, he maintained, there was only a single substantial form, namely the rational or intellectual soul. It was that soul which controlled the animal and vegetable functions of the body; and there was no need of a substantial form of corporality. If there was a plurality of forms, he argued, then it would not be the same entity, the same person, which both saw and thought. When a human being died there was nothing in common between the living person and his corpse other than the basic prime matter. It was this teaching of St Thomas which was condemned at Oxford in 1277. The doctrine of the plurality of forms was imposed upon the University.

Aquinas' teaching about the intellectual soul is the key to his psychology. The intellect, or intellectual soul, was peculiar to human beings. It was what marked them off from animals. The Latin word "*intellectus*" is connected with the verb "*intellegere*": this is commonly translated "understand", but in Aquinas' Latin it is a verb of very general use corresponding roughly to our word "think".

We employ the word "think" in two different ways: we talk of thinking *of* something, and we talk of thinking *that* something. Thus, in the first way, we may say that someone abroad thought of home, or thought of his family; in the second way we may say that someone thought that there was a prowler downstairs, or that inflation was on the increase. Aquinas makes a corresponding distinction between simple thoughts (thoughts *of*) and complex thoughts (thoughts *that*); both of these were acts of intellect. All thoughts, according to Aquinas, are expressible in language.

This does not mean that all thoughts are given public expression in words; I may mutter an insult behind clenched teeth, and some thoughts are not even put into words in the privacy of the imagination. The wanderer's thought of his family at breakfast may simply be an image of them sitting in the kitchen, not the internal enunciation of any proposition.

If the intellect is the capacity for thought, how can it be something peculiar to human beings? Surely a dog, seeing his master take the lead off the hook, thinks that he is going to be taken for a walk and expresses the thought quite clearly by leaping about? Aquinas does in fact allow animals the ability to think simple thoughts; but what is special to human beings is the relationship between thought and language. The intellect is best defined as the capacity for thinking those thoughts that only a language-user can think, thoughts for which no expression in non-linguistic behaviour can be conceived (e.g. the thought that truth is beauty or that there are stars many light-years away).

Aquinas believed that all the ideas of the intellect are in some way dependent on sense-experience; but the way in which he believed ideas to be abstracted from experience was a complicated one. The intellect was not one faculty, but two; or rather a single faculty with two powers: the agent intellect and the receptive intellect. It was the agent intellect which was the human capacity to abstract universal ideas from particular sense-experience; it was the receptive intellect which was the storehouse of those ideas once abstracted.

Aquinas postulated an agent intellect because he thought that the material objects of the world we lived in were not, in themselves, fit objects for intellectual understanding. A Platonic idea, universal, intangible, unchanging, unique, existing in a noetic heaven, might well be a suitable object for intellectual understanding; but there are no such things as Platonic ideas. Things in the physical world are in themselves, according to Aquinas, only potentially thinkable or intelligible. An animal with the same senses as ours perceives and deals with the same material objects as we do; but he cannot have intellectual thoughts about them or a scientific understanding of their nature, because he lacks the light cast by the agent intellect. We humans, because we can abstract ideas from the material conditions of the natural world, are able not just to perceive but to think about and understand the world.

Aquinas did not teach that the human intellect can know nothing but its own ideas; but he did believe that it was impossible to grasp material objects by a purely intellectual thought. The reason is that the principle of individuation for material objects is individual matter; and our intellect understands by abstracting ideas from such matter. But what is abstracted from individual matter is universal. So our intellect is not directly capable of knowing anything which is not universal. No matter how full a description I give of an individual, no matter what congeries of properties I ascribe to her, it is always logically possible that more than one individual satisfies the description and possesses the properties. Unless I bring in reference to particular times and places there may be no description I can give which could not in theory be satisfied by a human being other than the one I mean. I cannot individuate the person I mean simply by describing her appearance, her qualities. Only perhaps by pointing, or taking you to see her, or calling to mind an occasion on which we met, can I make clear beyond doubt which person I mean; and pointing and vision and this kind of memory are matters of sense, not of pure intellectual thought.

Intellectual knowledge of the individual, for Aquinas, must always be through cooperation between the intellect and the senses, by the joint use of our intellectual and sensory faculties, including imagination and memory. It is only by linking intellectual ideas with sensory experience that we know individuals and are capable of forming singular propositions such as "Socrates is a man". Aquinas called this relationship of the intellect to the sensory context of its activity "Reflection upon phantasms".

What are phantasms? From the role assigned to them in Aquinas' account of knowledge of individuals, it looks as if the notion of phantasm covers the whole of sense-experience: actual perception no less than imagination. Sometimes St Thomas writes as if he believed that whenever I am doing a bit of real seeing – e.g. looking at a beetle crawling across my desk – there is taking place, simultaneously, in my imagination, a replicating play of mental images representing a beetle crawling across my desk. If he really held this, I think he was wrong; but not in a way which damages his general account of knowledge of the individual.

Sometimes, too, he writes as if when we think of things in their absence, we do so by means of mental images of them; so that I think of the Statue of Liberty by picturing the Statue of Liberty. But there are a number of places where he qualifies this. He does indeed believe – and I think rightly – that we cannot think of things in their absence without using mental images: there has to be *something* going on in our imagination if we are to have a datable thought. But the mental image we use to think of X need not be mental pictures of X. This is a point made explicitly in relation to spiritual, unpicturable, entities like God. But it is true of picturable things too. Very commonly, when we think of things in their absence, the mental images used are the *words*, the imagined sounds and shapes of words in our fragmentary inner monologues.

Shut your eyes and think to yourself "water is H_2O". The words which echo in the silence of your imagination are *phantasmata*, imagined sounds. Without some such mental event as the subvocal mouthing of those words, there would be no reason to say you were thinking that thought, *now*. But what makes it a *thought*, and *that particular thought* is of course the meaning of the words and symbols. It is the understanding the words, the knowing the meaning, which makes what you do an act of *intellect*. The relation here between intellect and phantasm is necessary for any intellectual thought whatever, however universal. The "reflection upon phantasms" which we mentioned above adds something extra, in the case of knowledge of individuals. Thus, if the thought you think in silence is "Mrs Thatcher was a better administrator than President Reagan but not as good an actor" there is an extra role of sensory memory involved to attach the thoughts of Thatcher and Reagan to the individuals in question. We might put Aquinas' thought into Fregean mode by saying: Sense is a matter of intellect, reference is a matter of imagination.

For Aquinas the real object of all human knowledge is form. This is true both of sensory acquaintance and of intellectual understanding. The senses perceive the accidental forms of objects that are appropriate to each modality: with our eyes we see the colours and shapes of objects, with our noses we perceive their smells; colours shapes and smells are accidental forms. These are individual forms: the smell of *this rose*. Substantial form is not perceived by the senses, but grasped by the intellect. Material things are composed of matter and form: the individuality of a parcel of matter is not something that can be grasped by the intellect. The intellect can grasp what makes Socrates human, but not what makes him Socrates.

If Plato was wrong, as Aquinas thought he was, then there is not, outside the mind, any such thing as human nature as such: there is only the human nature of individual human beings such as Tom, Dick, and Harry. But because the humanity of individuals is form embedded in matter, it is not something which can, as such, be the object of pure intellectual thought. The agent intellect, on the basis of our experience of individual human beings, creates the intellectual object, humanity as such; but in order to conceive the humanity of Tom, Dick, or Harry we need to call in aid the imagination and the senses.

Aquinas' account of the agent intellect is complicated, and in some details obscure; but he is surely correct to attribute to human beings a special abstractive power unshared by other animals. In order to possess the type of concepts which we use to refer to and describe the objects of our experience it is not sufficient merely to have sensory experience. Children see, hear, and smell dogs before they acquire the concept *dog* and learn that the word "dog" can be applied to labradors, poodles and dachshunds but not to cats and sheep; they feel pricks and aches and cramps long before they acquire the concept *pain*. In mastering language the family baby acquires concepts which are beyond the reach of the family pets which are living in much the same sensory environment.

If the agent intellect is the capacity to acquire intellectual concepts and beliefs, the receptive intellect is the ability to retain and employ the concepts and beliefs thus acquired. It is the storehouse of ideas; the initially blank page on which the agent intellect writes. At any given moment in a human being's history there will be a repertoire of intellectual skills acquired and a stock of opinions and knowledge possessed. That repertoire and that stock make up the contents of the receptive intellect. Sometimes Aquinas' language makes us think of the receptive intellect as a kind of spiritual matter which takes on new forms as a thinker acquires new ideas. He warns us against taking this too seriously: but it is because of the Aristotelian comparison that to this day we speak of being *informed* about a matter and call the gaining of knowledge the acquisition of *information*.

Sense-perception, according to Aquinas, was, like the acquisition of intellectual information, a matter of the reception of forms in an immaterial manner. The sense takes in the colour of gold, without the gold. Forms thus received by the sense were stored in the fancy, and can be reshuffled to produce images of whatever we care to think about.

Aquinas' account of the relation between sense and imagination is, in various ways, unsatisfactory; but he had a clear grasp of the relationship between the intellect and the imagination when thought takes place in mental images or in subvocal speech. In such cases it is not the imagery that gives content to the intellectual thought; it is the intellect that gives meaning to the imagery – whether imagined words or mental pictures – by using it in a certain way and in a certain context. In the book of our thoughts, it is the intellect that provides the text; the mental images are only illustrations.

Sense-perception and intellectual thought are, then, both cases of the reception of forms in a more or less immaterial manner in the mind. In both perception and thought a form exists, as Aquinas puts it, "intentionally". When I see the redness of the setting sun, redness exists intentionally in my vision; when I think of the roundness of the earth, roundness exists in my intellect. In each case the form exists without the matter to which it is joined in reality: the sun itself does not enter into my eye, nor does the earth, with all its mass, move into my intellect.

Suppose I think of a horse. There are two questions which a philosopher might ask about this thought. First: what makes it a thought *of a horse*? Second, what makes it *my* thought? Aquinas' answer to the first question is that it is the very same thing as makes a real horse a horse: namely, the form of horse. The form exists, individualized and materialized, in the real horse; it exists, universal and immaterial, in my mind. In the one case it has natural existence; in the other case it has intentional existence.

Aquinas' answer to the second question is less clear cut. There is nothing in the content of a thought that makes it one person's thought rather than another. Innumerable people besides myself believe that two and two make four: when I believe this, what makes the belief *my* belief? In response to the question, Aquinas points to the connection between the intellectual content of the thought (which is universal) and the mental images in which it is embodied (which are peculiar to me). The validity of the answer clearly depends upon the theory of the single human form: the intellectual and sensory activity must both be exercises of a single set of abilities if the thought is to be attached to a person.

If Aquinas' answer is to be fully convincing it needs to be spelt out more fully than he ever does. But what is notable is that unlike later philososphers he does not relate thought to a self or ego. This, in my view, is all to the good: the belief that each of us has a self is a piece of philosophers' nonsense. I and myself are one; myself is what I am, not a self which I have. If it were, then what in heaven's name is the I who has the self? My self is not a part of me, not even a most elusive, intimate, and precious part of me. The belief in a self which is different from the human being whose self it is is a grammatical illusion generated by the reflexive pronoun. It is as if a philosopher was puzzled what the property of "own-ness" was which my own room possesses in addition to the property of being mine. When, outside philosophy, I talk about myself, I am simply talking about the human being, Anthony Kenny; and my self is nothing other than myself. It is a philosophical muddle to allow the space which differentiates "my self" from "myself" to generate the illusion of a mysterious metaphysical entity distinct from, but obscurely linked to, the human being who is talking to you.

The grammatical error which is the essence of the theory of the self is a deep error and one which is not generated by mistaken grammar alone. The illusion has a number of different roots, of which the most important are the epistemological root and the psychological root.

The epistemological root of the notion of the self is Cartesian scepticism. Descartes, in the *Meditations*, convinces himself that he can doubt whether the world exists and whether he has a body. He then goes on to argue, "I can doubt whether I have a body; but I cannot doubt whether I exist; for what is this I which is doubting". The "I" must refer to something of which is body is no part, and hence to something which is no more than a part of the human being Descartes. The Cartesian ego is a substance whose essence is pure thought, the mind or *res cogitans*.

The psychological root of the notion of the self derives from the idea that imagination is an interior sense. The self, as conceived in the empiricist tradition of Locke, is the subject of inner sensation. The self is the eye of inner vision, the ear of inner hearing, or rather, it is the mythical possessor of both inner eye and inner ear and whatever other inner organs of sensation may be fantasized.

The self, to be sure, is a topic which has fascinated other people beside philosophers. Gerard Manley Hopkins, in an often quoted passsage of his treatise on St Ignatius' spiritual exercises, wrote as follows:

> We may learn that all things are created by consideration of the world without or of ourselves the world within. The former is the consideration commonly dwelt on, but the latter takes on the mind more hold. I find myself both as man and as myself something most determined and distinctive, at pitch, more distinctive and higher pitched than anything else I see; I find myself with my pleasures and pains, my powers and my experiences, my deserts and guilt, my shame and sense of beauty, my dangers, hopes, fears and all my fate, more important to myself than anything I see . . .

And this is much more true when we consider the mind; when I consider my selfbeing, my consciousness and feeling of myself, that taste of myself, of *I* and *me* above and in all things, which is more distinctive than the taste of ale or alum, more distinctive than the smell of walnutleaf or camphor, and is incommunicable by any means to another man (as when I was a child I used to ask myself: What must it be to be someone else?) Nothing else in nature comes near this unspeakable stress of pitch, distinctiveness, and selving, this selfbeing of my own. Nothing explains it or resembles it, except so far as this, that other men to themselves have the same feeling. But this only multiplies the phenomena to be explained so far as the cases are like and do resemble. But to me there is no resemblance: searching nature I taste *self* but at one tankard, that of my own being.

Like Hopkins, David Hume looked within to find his self; notoriously Hume's most diligent introspection failed to reveal any such thing.

When I enter most intimately into what I call *myself* I always stumble on some particular perception or other, of heat or cold, light or shade, love or hatred, pain or pleasure. I never catch *myself* at any time without a perception, and never can observe anything but the perception.

The self is everywhere – as for Hopkins – or it is nowhere – as for Hume. This is because the self is a mythical entity. A taste of which everything tasted would not be a taste, since taste is a faculty of discrimination; a self which is perceived no matter what is perceived is no better than a self which is not perceived at all.

There is, of course, such a thing as self-knowledge; but it is not knowledge of a self. When I know myself, what I know is myself, not my self. But even without the surd of the self, self-knowledge is a difficult philosophical topic: and it is instructive to see the difficulties which it presents for Aquinas even though he is blessedly free from belief in a mythical self.

Aquinas' general theory of knowledge, we have seen, makes intellectual knowledge of any individual problematic. The reason is that the principle of individuation for material objects is individual matter; and our intellect understands by abstracting ideas from such

41

matter. But what is abstracted from individual matter is universal. So our intellect is not directly capable of knowing anything which is not universal. If this is so, how can I have intellectual knowledge of myself? According to Aquinas I am neither a disembodied spirit nor a universal, but a human being, an individual material object. As an individual material substance, it seems, I can be no fit object for intellectual cognition.

As we have seen, Aquinas solved the problem in relation to other individuals by appealing to the sensory context of thought. My relationship to other individuals is intellectual, because I can apply to them the universal ideas which are expressed in our common language; it is sensory because only the context of sense-experience enables us to attach the universal predicates to the individual subjects.

Aquinas' theory here seemed unnecessarily complicated to his successor Duns Scotus and to other philosophers, medieval and modern, who have believed in individuating essences, or, to use the Scotist term, haecceities. A haecceity is sufficiently like a form to be at home in the intellect: for Scotus the intellect can grasp the individuality of a thing by taking in its haecceity along with its universal form. But I believe that St Thomas was right to reject the notion of individuating essences: they are a misguided attempt to combine the logical features of form and matter, of predicate and subject. St Thomas did, of course, believe in individual essences – the essence of Peter is numerically distinct from the essence of Paul – but individual essences are not individuating essences. Peter's essence is a human nature individuated by being the essence *of Peter*; it is not Peter who is individuated by some Petreity which is his essence.

If there were forms such as Petreity it would be as true of them as it is of forms of other kinds that one cannot individuate by the accumulation of form: it must remain logically possible for more than one thing to posses identical Petreities. Once again, this thought received eloquent expression by Hopkins, that most engaging and intrepid Scotist.

> In the world, besides natures, or essences, or inscapes, and the selves, supposits, or hypostases, or, in the case of rational natures, persons that wear and "fetch" or instance them, there is still something else – fact or fate. For let natures be A,B, . . . Y,Z, and supposits or selves a,b, . . . y,z: then if a is capable of A,B, . . . Y,Z (singly or together) and receives, say A, if b capable of the same receives A and if

c capable of the same receives M, so that we have aA, bA, cM, these combinations are three arbitrary or absolute facts, not depending on any essential relation between a & A, b & A or c & M but on the will of the Creator. Further, a & b are in the same nature A. But a uses it well and is saved, b ill and is damned; these are two facts, two fates, not depending on the relation between a and b on the one hand and A on the other. Now as the difference of the fact and fate does not depend on A, which is the same for both, it must depend on a and b. So that selves are from the first intrinsically different. (op. cit. p. 146)

In other words, Scotist selves have to be individuated in advance of possessing the haecceities which individuate them. But that takes away the point of introducing haecceities in the first place. The *reductio ad absurdum* is complete.

By contrast, Aquinas' theory of intellectual knowledge of the individual is basically sound, and much preferable to its Scotist alternatives, old and new. It is, however, bound up with a dubious theory of the imagination as an inner sense. Aquinas seems to have thought that an inner sense differed from an outer sense principally in having an organ and an object inside the body instead of outside the body; and he sometimes writes implicitly – as Descartes was later to write explicitly – as if mental images were images in the brain. This seems to me an error; but I believe that one can tacitly correct these errors and be left with a theory which is both philosophically defensible and recognizably Thomist.

The situation changes, however, if we turn from knowledge of other individuals to knowledge of oneself. Here, I shall claim, the weaknesses of St Thomas' account of the phantasm affect the substance of the theory; and once the account is adjusted to remove the weaknesses, the theory of self-knowledge reveals itself as inadequate.

A criticism can be levelled at Aquinas which he himself levelled at Averroes. Averroes, St Thomas says, regarded the receptive intellect as a separate substance, and "said that the thoughts of that separate substance were my thoughts or your thoughts to the extent that that possible intellect was linked to me or to you by the phantasms which are in me or you". The way in which this happened was thus explained by Averroes.

The intellectual idea which is united to the possible intellect as its form and act has two subjects – one the phantasm, the other the receptive intellect. Thus the receptive intellect is linked to us through its form by means of the phantasm; and that is how, when the possible intellect thinks, the human being thinks.

This account, St Thomas says, is empty. He gives three reasons against it, of which the third is the clinching one. Let us allow, he says, that one and the same idea is both a form of the possible intellect and is simultaneously in the phantasm; just as a wall's looking blue to me is the very same thing as my seeing the blueness of the wall.

But the coloured wall, whatever sense impression it makes on the sight is seen, not seeing; it is the animal with the visual faculty on which the impression is made that is doing the seeing. But this is the alleged kind of link between the possible intellect and the human being in whom are the phantasms whose ideas are in the possible intellect – the same kind of link as that between the coloured wall and the sight on which the colour is impressed. But the wall doesn't see, but is seen; so it would follow not that the human being thought, but that his phantasms were thought of by the possible intellect.

St Thomas's criticism of Averroes seems to me inescapable; but does his own account of knowledge of self fare any better?

St Thomas in fact gives more than one account of self-knowledge. His fullest, and most considered answer to the question how the intellect knows its own essence is summarized thus:

It is not by its essence but by its acts that the intellect knows itself. And this in two ways. First, in particular, as when Socrates or Plato perceives himself to have an intellectual soul from the fact that he perceives himself thinking intellectual thoughts. Secondly, in general, as when we consider the nature of the human mind from the nature of the intellectual activity.

Here "Socrates' intellect knows itself" is glossed, in conformity with Aristotelian orthodoxy "Socrates perceives himself to have an intellectual soul"; and the theorem stated is an instance of the axiom that faculties are known by their actions.

Thus, Aquinas says, everything is known so far as actual; and the perfection of the intellect is its own immanent action. The human intellect is not, like the divine intellect, identical with its own act, nor does it have, like an angelic intellect, its own essence as its primary object. Its primary object is the nature of material things.

> Therefore, what is first known by the human intellect is this object; then, in the second place, the act by which the object is known is itself known; and finally, by way of the act, the intellect, of which the act of thinking is the perfection, is itself known.

So the intellect knows itself by knowing its own acts. But what makes these acts – thoughts, exercises of concepts and beliefs – the acts of an individual? We must put to St Thomas the question he put to Averroes.

Aquinas was right to say, against Averroes, that my thoughts are *my* thoughts because they are thoughts of the intellectual soul which is individuated by my body. But when we ask for an account of what makes the soul *that* soul, what is its relation to my body which individuates it, we seem to be given no satisfactory answer. For the mind (the possible intellect) is the locus of universal ideas, concepts, and beliefs; there is nothing in their content which relates them to this body. And the way in which the body is related to the thoughts is not by being an instrument in their acquisition or exercise. St Thomas is anxious to say that thought is an activity of the soul alone, and that the soul, having an independent activity, is capable also of independent existence, as an incorruptible substance in its own right.

The way in which the body is involved in intellectual thought, for Aquinas, is simply that my beliefs are acquired and employed with the aid of phantasms generated by my brain. But if so, the body is necessary for intellectual activity not in order to provide the mind with an instrument, but only to provide the mind with an object – phantasms being, in one sense of the word "object", the object of the intellect's activity.

But if this is correct, then my body is related to my thought only in a relation of efficient causality – as Leonardo is related to the Mona Lisa, or as the blue wall is related to my vision. And this, as Aquinas said against Averroes, is not enough. Leonardo does not see the painting he left behind, nor does the wall see its colour.

What is the correct account of the relation of the body to thought? Aquinas is right to say that my thoughts are *my* thoughts because they are thoughts of the mind which is the mind of my body. Where he goes wrong is in his account of what it is to be the mind of a particular body. The correct answer is that a mind is the mind of the body whose actions *express* that mind's thoughts. My thoughts are the thoughts which find expression in the words and actions of my body; your thoughts are the thoughts which find expression in what is done by your body. It is by looking to see whose hand wrote certain words, whose lips formed certain sounds, that we decide *whose* thoughts are expressed in writings on paper or sounds in the air. It is by observing the performance of Socrates' body that we discover what intellectual skills, or moral virtues, Socrates possesses. And this is not a contingent matter – it is not an inductive procedure we adopt to discover the contents of a mind by observing the behaviour of a body. The relevant bodily behaviour is, in Wittgenstein's words, a criterion for the possession of the mental skills and dispositions.

In our own case, of course, we do not have to use criteria to discover what our thoughts are. As St Thomas says, we perceive ourselves to think. I know *what* I am thinking, and I know that it is I who am thinking, without needing to base this judgement on criteria. But *what* I know when I know that I have a certain thought is the *same* as what others know when they know what I am thinking; and *what* they know and what I know is something intrinsically linked to bodily criteria.

But the link with bodily criteria is not the crude and simple one of behaviourist fantasy. Much of our thought takes place in private meditation and finds no bodily expression. (We may be grateful for this: a world in which everyone always expressed their thoughts would be noisy, boring, and cruel.) So the question remains: what is the relation to my body of the thoughts which I think silently in the privacy of my imagination – that is to say, the phantasms which St Thomas takes as the crucial link between body and mind in thought?

It is no doubt true, as St Thomas says, that the occurrence of phantasms is due, causally, to events in the brain. But that causal link is contingent and not necessary, and it is not enough to make the thoughts *thought by me*, as St Thomas himself said in his polemic against Averroes.

The truth seems to be that what makes my unexpressed thoughts *my* thoughts is that they are thoughts which, if they found expression, would be expressed by my body (this body). It is I who would have to answer the question "a penny for your thoughts" by someone who wished to know what I was thinking; it is to this body the request must be addressed.

What *sense* the thoughts in my mind have depends on *my* mastery of the language in which they occur, in my decoding of the symbols and imagery in which they are embodied. What *reference* they have depends on the history of *this body*, making the links between the current image and the remembered events which provide the context for the reflection upon phantasms. The very fact that they are unexpressed is something which depends on my will. As we grow from babyhood, expressed thoughts come first; the repression of their public expression is a social skill learned later with difficulty as inculcated by parents. While unspoken thoughts are episodic in that they are datable events (like a pang of hunger), they are also dispositional in that (again like a pang of hunger) they are defined by the kind of expression to which they have an intrinsic relationship. So even in our most secret thoughts the relationship between mind and body is more than the mere causal interaction which St Thomas' theory suggests. The notion of expression, not that of causation, is the key to the mind–body relationship. We must add Wittgenstein to Aquinas if we are to save Aquinas from falling despite himself into the arms of Averroes.

Let us return, finally, to the Oxford condemnation of Aquinas. It might well seem, initially that the question whether in human beings there were multiple forms or only a single intellectual soul was something only peripheral to St Thomas' psychology, and of little interest to twentieth-century philosophy. But we have now seen how the question of the relationship between the intellectual and the sensory powers permeates every aspect of St Thomas' philosophy of the mind and its relation to the body. Moreover, the condemned propositions link up with present-day concerns about the nature of personal identity and with currently debated issues in medical ethics.

At the present time some philosophers regard memory as the key to personal identity; others see bodily continuity as its essence, while others again present theories which use both memory and bodily continuity as criteria. Those who separate personal identity from bodily identity take the side of those medievals who argued for the plurality of forms; those who identify the two in effect subscribe to the thesis for which St Thomas was condemned.

The questions debated in Oxford in 1277 are not mere abstract issues of no practical relevance. They connect with fundamental problems about the beginning and end of individual human life.

What is the right way to conceptualize the continuity between a foetus and a baby? Should the continuance of vegetative function in an unconscious human body be taken as an indication of the permanence of a rational soul bearing the rights of persons? Taking sides in the medieval debate goes hand in hand with the approach to be adopted in answering these difficult questions.

In 1325 the Bishop of Paris proclaimed that the censure his university had passed in 1277 had no canonical value so far as it concerned St Thomas. In 1914 Pope Pius X listed as a thesis which was safe and sound to be taught in Catholic schools, "The same rational soul is united to the body in such a way that it is its one and only substantial form, and through it a human being is animal, living, bodily, and substantial."

Rome and Paris have withdrawn their initial condemnation of Aquinas. Only Oxford, so far as I know, has not yet done so. In presenting his views in this chapter, therefore, I may perhaps have rendered myself liable to lose my MA.

References

Aquinas, Thomas (1993) *Selected Philosophical Writings*, ed. T. McDermott, Oxford: Oxford University Press, The World's Classics.
Kenny, Anthony (1993) *Aquinas on Mind*, London: Routledge.
Davies, Brian, OP (1992) *The Thought of Thomas Aquinas*, Oxford: Oxford University Press.

4

THE SOUL IN GREEK CHRISTIANITY

Kallistos Ware

An unexplored country

'Know yourself.' The words inscribed on the temple of Apollo at Delphi are often repeated by Greek Christian authors. 'The greatest of all lessons is to know yourself,' states Clement of Alexandria (*c.*150–*c.*215). 'For if someone knows himself, he will know God; and if he knows God, he will become like God.'[1] Self-knowledge signifies God-knowledge, and God-knowledge in its turn leads to God-likeness. Such self-knowledge, however, as Greek thinkers whether Christian or non-Christian readily acknowledged, is no easy task. For what in fact is my real and true self? More specifically, what is my soul? 'I have a soul', observes Cyril of Jerusalem (*c.*315–87), 'and yet I cannot describe its characteristics.'[2] John Chrysostom (*c.*347–407) agrees. 'The essence of our own soul is not known to us fully, or rather it is not known to us at all.'[3] Cyril and Chrysostom would have found no fault with the observation of C. G. Jung that the psyche is 'a foreign, almost unexplored country'.[4]

Significantly Gregory of Nyssa (*c.*330–*c.*395) provides a specific reason for this mysterious, indefinable character of our inner self. The human being, he says, is made in the image and likeness of God, as Scripture affirms (Gen. 1: 26–7) ; each of us is a created icon of the uncreated God. Since God is incomprehensible, so also is the human person: 'An image is only truly such in so far as it expresses all the attributes of its archetype. . . . One of the characteristics of the divine nature is to be in its essence beyond our understanding; it is altogether necessary, then, for the image to resemble the archetype in this respect.'[5] Negative or apophatic theology requires as its counterpart an apophatic anthropology. Who am I? I do not really know. Even the great Origen (*c.*185–*c.*254),

49

so his follower Pamphilus reports, never dared to write a treatise on the human soul;[6] he regarded the task as beyond his powers.

How are we to gain a better understanding of this continuing mystery of our human personhood? Almost without exception, Greek Christian thinkers from New Testament times to the end of the Byzantine era – the first to the fifteenth century – are in agreement on at any rate one point. In order to understand ourselves, theory alone – philosophical speculation, abstract doctrinal definitions – is never by itself sufficient. Practice or *ascesis* is also required. Self-knowledge can only be gained through prayer and worship, through sharing in the sacraments and through inner stillness. In this *ascesis* the body also plays its part, through fasting and prostrations, through symbolic actions such as the sign of the Cross, and through the psychosomatic technique employed in conjunction with the Jesus Prayer or Invocation of the Holy Name. Without ascetic practice of this kind, both inner and outer, we cannot begin to understand our soul.

An undivided unity in the divine image

Since our human nature is in this way beyond our full comprehension, it is scarcely surprising that there should be in Greek Christian authors no single, agreed definition of the soul. 'The subject of the soul is differently handled by almost every ancient author,' remarks Nemesius of Emesa (late fourth century).[7] He is speaking here of the non-Christian philosophers, but his words also apply to the Christian tradition. Some Greek Fathers are content to offer a definition of the soul that is basically Platonist: 'a living and intellectual essence. . . . non-material and bodiless', says Gregory of Nyssa;[8] 'an intellectual essence that is bodiless, passionless and immortal', state the *Questions to Antiochus*, attributed (incorrectly) to Athanasius of Alexandria (*c.*296–373).[9] Most authors prefer a wide-ranging and inclusive description. Thus the *Spiritual Homilies* (late fourth century) attributed to Macarius the Egyptian equate the soul broadly with 'the inner man' (*ho esō anthropos*),[10] treating it as a diversity-in-unity: 'Just as the members of the body, though many, are said to be a single human being, so also the members of the soul are many – intellect (*nous*), conscience, will, thoughts – . . . but the soul is one.'[11]

Even though it is difficult to find definitive statements about the soul in Greek Christianity, there is none the less a widespread consensus on two points. First, almost all Greek Christian authors

50

emphasize the affirmation in Genesis 1: 26–7 that our soul or personhood is created 'in the image of God'. Second, body and soul are normally seen as two complementary entities that constitute an undivided unity; neither can properly exist apart from the other, and their separation at death is no more than temporary. Let us take these two points in order.

In the first place, then, it is generally accepted by all Christian thinkers – and this, of course, includes the Latin West as well as the Greek and Syriac East – that the decisive element in our human personhood, that which distinguishes us humans from the animals and makes us unique within the entire created order, is precisely the fact that we are constituted in the divine image. But immediately a difficulty arises. While it is taken for granted that we are in the divine image, in no authoritative source – neither in the Bible, nor in the Nicene–Constantinopolitan Creed (381), nor yet in the doctrinal decrees of the seven Ecumenical Councils (325–787) – do we find any clear statement specifying the precise nature of this indwelling 'image'. 'Tradition holds that every human being is in the image of God, but it does not attempt to define in what aspect of the person this image should be located', observes Epiphanius of Salamis (c.315–403). ' . . . It cannot be denied that all humans are in the image of God, but we do not enquire too curiously *how* they are in the image.'[12]

Most Greek Christian writers in fact link the divine image with the soul, and exclude the body from participation in it. But, while this is the majority opinion, it is not the universal view; for there is a significant minority that associates the divine image with the total human being, body, soul and spirit together. Irenaeus of Lyons (c.130–c.200) is a noteworthy exponent of this second standpoint.[13] More particularly, the divine image is regularly connected with the possession by humans of self-awareness and reason, of freedom and moral choice, and of dominion over the animals (Gen. 1: 28).

Underlying these specific characteristics, there is a more fundamental truth implied in the notion of the divine image: it signifies a *relationship*. The human soul or person, because it is in the divine image, cannot be truly understood on its own, as a self-contained and autonomous reality. It can be understood only in terms of its relationship with God. To say, 'My soul is created in God's image', is to say, 'I have the divine as the determining element in my humanness; God is at the innermost core of my being; apart from God I am unintelligible.' For this reason, from the viewpoint of Greek Christianity any attempted analysis of the human soul which describes it in isolation, without reference to God, is bound to seem fatally defective. Leaving out of account our relationship with the divine, we have overlooked the one element which, above all else, renders the human soul distinctive and, indeed, unique.

Because the human soul is in God's image, it also follows that the freedom conferred on us by the presence of this image is not an arbitrary and unrestricted freedom. We are authentically free according to the divine image and likeness only if we exercise our freedom in conformity to God's will, this is to say, only if in our acts of free choice we reflect divine love and compassion.

Turning now to the second point, the integral unity of soul and body, we find that here at least there are two clear authoritative statements in Greek Christianity:

1   The fifth Ecumenical Council, meeting at Constantinople in 553, in its condemnation of Origen formally denied the pre-existence of the soul.[14] Soul and body come into existence at the same time.

2   Following the New Testament, the Nicene–Constantinopolitan Creed (381) concludes, 'I await the resurrection of the body.' The severance of the soul from the body at physical death is not final and irrevocable, for the two will be united once again at Christ's second coming on the last day, and thereafter they will coexist eternally in the age to come. Christianity, that is to say, does not believe simply in the immortality of the soul, but it affirms the ultimate reintegration of the *total* person, soul and body together.

If we look for the basis of this faith in the resurrection of the body, then we find that it does not derive from any particular philosophical theory about the soul–body relationship, but it is founded upon what the early Christians and their successors regard as an historical fact: the resurrection of Jesus Christ from the dead on the third day. As Paul argues in 1 Corinthians 15: 20–4, our conviction that we shall all eventually be raised from the dead depends upon our belief that Christ has already been so raised. Christ has marked out the path that we in turn shall follow: he is the 'first fruits', to use Paul's term, and we are the harvest.

The Gospel accounts of the resurrection make it clear that Christ was raised from the dead not in a new body but in the same body as he had before; thus the disciples recognize him precisely by seeing the wounds of the Cross on his hands and feet and in his side (John

20: 20–8). Since Christ's resurrection forms the foundation and paradigm of our own future resurrection, it follows from this that we too, at our resurrection on the last day, will have a body that is in some significant sense the same as our present body. There will be a genuine continuity. Although the saints will rise in a body that is glorified and transfigured – a 'spiritual ' body, as Paul puts it (1 Cor. 15: 44) – 'spiritual' in this context does not signify 'non-material'. They will rise in *this* physical body which they now have.

Yet, while affirming continuity, most Greek Fathers wisely refrain from attempting to explain in too much detail what is the exact connection between our present body and the body that we shall receive at our resurrection. In some authors, it is true, the connection is understood in a close and literal sense. 'At the resurrection', state the *Spiritual Homilies* of Macarius, 'all the members of the body are raised; not a hair perishes.'[15] Other writers, such as Gregory of Nyssa, adopt a more carefully qualified approach. During our present life, Gregory points out, the constituent elements making up our physical body are constantly changing; but the soul imposes upon these elements a particular 'form' (*eidos*) and by virtue of the uninterrupted preservation of this 'form' it may legitimately be asserted that we continue throughout our life to have the same body. At the resurrection the soul will reassemble the particles of matter from which its body was formed during this present life, and it will once more impress upon these particles the same 'form' as before. Thus our resurrection body will be, in a genuinely recognizable way, the same body as that which we possess at present.[16]

Gregory of Nyssa seems to assume that at the final resurrection the soul will gather together, from the common store of matter, precisely the selfsame physical particles as previously constituted its body. In the light of current scientific theories concerning the nature of matter, it is difficult to give any clear meaning to such an assertion. But, in any case, surely there is no need for Gregory to assert in this way that the resurrection body must necessarily be formed from the individual particles that now compose it. It would be enough for his purpose to say that the 'form' imposed by the soul remains the same. The important thing is not the identity of the material constituents but the continuity of the 'form' supplied by the soul. C. S. Lewis appeals in this context to the example of a waterfall. The drops in a waterfall are continually changing, but the curve assumed by the water remains constant; since the water preserves the same 'form', it is indeed the same waterfall.[17]

The two authoritative statements mentioned above – the first from the fifth Ecumenical Council, denying the pre-existence of the soul, and the second from the Creed, affirming the final resurrection of the body – clearly imply, when taken together, a holistic view of the human person. If the body and soul of each human being come into existence simultaneously, and if they will be reunited at the final resurrection of the created order, then it follows that they together constitute an integral whole, an undivided unity. A Platonist may willingly affirm, 'The soul is man';[18] but to this a Christian whether Greek or Latin is bound to respond, in the words of Aquinas: 'The soul is not the whole man, and my soul is not me.'[19] What I call 'me' is not my soul without my body, nor my body without my soul, but the combination and coinherence of the two together.[20] Beyond this basic affirmation of the fundamental unity of soul and body, the official doctrinal definitions of Eastern Christendom do not go.

Distinguer pour unir

While insisting that the person is an integral whole, Greek Christian writers are at the same time willing to distinguish various subdivisions within this all-embracing unity. Most of the schemes which they adopt lack originality, derived as they are from Classical Greek philosophy.

First, as regards the *total person*, some Patristic texts presuppose a bipartite scheme, affirming a simple contrast between soul and body. This is the case, for example, with the definition adopted at the Council of Chalcedon (451), which states that the incarnate Christ is 'complete in Godhead and complete in humanity, truly God and truly man [formed] from a rational soul and a body';[21] here the 'rational soul' and the 'body' are clearly envisaged as constituting what it is to be man (*anthropos*) or a human being.

Other sources prefer a tripartite scheme, making a distinction between the soul, on the one hand, and the intellect (*nous*) or spirit (*pneuma*) on the other, so that the human person is regarded as a triunity of intellect, soul and body. Origen, for example, is a convinced trichotomist, insisting that the human being consists of 'soul, body and vital spirit';[22] the third element, the human spirit, he treats as definitely distinct from the Holy Spirit of God (in Irenaeus the distinction is less clear). Origen claims a Biblical basis for this tripartite scheme: 'Throughout Scripture I observe a distinction between soul and spirit.'[23]

Besides those authors who are consistently dichotomist or consistently trichotomist, there are others who alternate between the one scheme and the other, evidently considering that there is no basic discrepancy between the two. Apollinaris of Laodicea (*c.*310–*c.*390) is a case in point.[24]

Pace Origen, it may be doubted whether either the trichotomist or the dichotomist scheme has a clear basis in Scripture. The Hebraic concept of personhood, as found in the Old Testament, is embodied and physical: scarcely if ever is there a soul–body contrast of the Platonic type, but the person is seen as a single unity of 'flesh-animated-by-soul'. In the New Testament Paul nowhere makes a direct contrast between body and soul, although he often distinguishes between flesh (*sarx*) and spirit (*pneuma*). It is true that on one occasion he uses the triad 'spirit and soul and body' (1 Thess. 5: 23), but it may be doubted whether he intends here to provide a systematic enumeration of the 'parts' or 'components' of the human person. Many post-Biblical writers in Greek Christianity, unlike Paul, do indeed draw heavily on the Platonic soul–body contrast, but few if any among them go as far as Platonism does in treating the two as distinct entities whose destiny is to be separated.[25] Even Origen, who was condemned for teaching the pre-existence of the soul, found it necessary to allow some place in the *eschaton* for the resurrection of the body.[26]

Second, as regards the *soul*, Greek Christian authors employ a variety of classifications, sometimes twofold and sometimes threefold. Clement of Alexandria makes a subdivision within the soul between 'knowledge' (*gnōsis*) and 'impulse' (*hormē*), that is to say, between the cognitive and the affective/volitional parts of the soul.[27] Basil of Caesarea (*c.*300–*c.*379) employs the Aristotelian distinction between the 'active' and the 'passive' or 'receptive' aspects of the soul.[28]

More frequently, however, the Greek Fathers adopt the tripartite subdivision of the soul, developed by Plato:[29]

logistikon, the 'rational' or 'intellectual' aspect;
thymikon, the 'spirited' or 'incensive' aspect;
epithymētikon, the 'appetitive' or 'desiring' aspect.[30]

Origen, however, expresses reservations about this classification, noting with good reason that it lacks support from Scripture.[31]

A second tripartite scheme popular among the Greek Fathers – likewise with little explicit support from Scripture – is the subdivision found in Aristotle:[32]

the vegetable soul (nutritive);
the animal soul (sensitive);
the human soul (rational/intellectual).

In this threefold Aristotelian scheme – used for instance by Gregory of Nyssa[33] – it is at once evident that the term *psychē* is being used with a connotation far wider than that normally ascribed today to the word 'soul'; it signifies not just self-consciousness but, in a broader sense, vital energy or life-force. If we follow Aristotle, then we shall ascribe 'soul' (in some sense of the word) to animals. But Gregory of Nyssa adds that in the strict sense it is only the human, rational soul that can properly be designated by the term *psychē*; the animal soul, and still more the vegetable soul, is not a soul in the true sense.[34] In that case, animals do not really have souls. This is a question to which we shall return shortly.

An integrating symbol: the heart

While using subdivisions of this kind, the Greek Fathers, following Plato,[35] at the same time insist that the soul is fundamentally one. But, as we have seen, in their insistence upon unity they go further than Plato by affirming, with varying degrees of emphasis, that the soul is not only one with itself but also one with the body. To indicate this all-embracing wholeness of the human person many of them employ, as an integrating symbol, the notion of the heart (*kardia*).[36] There may sometimes be Stoic elements in this Greek Patristic understanding of the heart, but the primary source is the Bible.

Today the heart is normally contrasted with the head; while the head is regarded as the seat of the reason, the heart is seen as the realm of the emotions and affections. Presumably the late Duchess of Windsor understood 'heart' in this sense when she entitled her memoirs *The Heart has its Reasons*. She was of course quoting Pascal,[37] although it may be doubted whether he intended by the heart exactly what she meant. In the Bible, on the other hand, the heart has a far broader connotation: it designates, not simply the affections and emotions (these are located primarily in the guts or belly), but rather the spiritual centre of the total human person. There is in the Old and New Testaments no head–heart contrast. The heart is the seat of memory, of the conscience, of thought, wisdom and intelligence. It is the place where we make moral decisions and where we experience divine grace. God dwells in the heart, and so also (if we allow him) does Satan.[38]

In some Greek Patristic texts, such as the writings ascribed to Dionysius the Areopagite (*c.*500), there are very few references to the heart, and when it is mentioned no special significance is attached to the term. But other sources, such as the Macarian *Homilies*, ascribe to the heart the centrality and the richness of meaning that it possesses in the Bible. 'The heart', state the *Homilies*, 'directs and governs the whole bodily organism; and when grace possesses the pasturages of the heart, it rules over all the members and the thoughts. For there, in the heart, is the intellect (*nous*), and all the thoughts of the soul and its expectation; and in this way grace penetrates throughout all parts of the body.'[39]

Here the heart signifies, first of all, the physical organ located in our chest, but at the same time it denotes symbolically far more than this. It is, to use the Hindu term, a *chakra*, a centre of spiritual energy, and not just a part of our body. It is regarded as the directing centre of the total human person, as the place where we think, where the *nous* dwells, and where divine grace is active. It is the point of convergence between the body and the soul, and at the same time the meeting-place between the human being and God. The heart, as understood by the *Homilies*, even corresponds in some measure to the modern concept of the unconscious: 'Within the heart is an unfathomable depth,' states the author.[40]

The Greek Patristic tradition concerning the heart is lucidly summed up, towards the end of the Byzantine era, by Gregory Palamas (1296–1359). He points out that some Fathers locate the mind (*dianoia*) or the intellect (*nous*) in the head, and others in the heart. This seeming discrepancy does not greatly disturb him, for he considers that there are no dogmas in the realm of physiology. In any case, since the mind is non-material, it cannot be precisely located in space: citing John Climacus (*c.*570–*c.*649), he says that our mind is 'both in us and not in us'. 'We know very well', argues Palamas, 'that our intelligence (*logistikon*) is neither within us as in a container – for it is incorporeal – nor yet outside us, for it is united to us.'

Palamas himself, however, expresses a definite preference for the approach found in the Macarian *Homilies* (which he quotes), whereby the mind or intellect is associated with the heart rather than the head. He describes the heart as 'the shrine of the intelligence and the chief intellectual organ of the body. . . . the ruling organ . . . the throne of grace, where the intellect and all the thoughts of the soul reside'. Our aim in prayer, he says, is to 'collect our intellect, outwardly dispersed through the senses, and bring it back within ourselves – back to the heart itself, the shrine of the thoughts'. Hesychasts – those who pursue inner stillness (*hesychia*) through the practice of contemplative prayer – strive therefore 'to bring their intellect back and to enclose it within their body, and particularly within that innermost body within the body that we call the heart'.[41]

In this connection Palamas defends the psychosomatic technique used by certain Hesychasts when reciting the Jesus Prayer (a short invocation of the Holy Name of Jesus, usually in the form 'Lord Jesus Christ, Son of God, have mercy on me'). The Hesychasts adopted during prayer a crouching posture, with their gaze fixed on the heart or navel, and they linked the words of the Jesus Prayer with the rhythm of their breathing; at the same time they practised an inner exploration, striving to make their intellect descend into their heart. Because of this technique, their critics styled them *omphalopsychoi*, 'navel-psychics', people who locate the soul in the navel, a *sobriquet* which the Hesychasts themselves vehemently repudiated. Palamas, invoking the principle, 'After the fall our inner being naturally adapts itself to outward forms',[42] regards this Hesychast technique as legitimate, although he does not attach fundamental importance to it. Clearly, then, Palamas envisages a certain correlation between the organs of our physical body and the different centres of spiritual energy within us; there is between the two what has appropriately been termed a relationship of 'analogy-participation'.[43] But he does not interpret this correlation or analogy in an unduly literal manner.

This interpretation of the heart, found in the Macarian *Homilies*, Palamas and other Greek Fathers, has many similarities with the understanding of *memoria* in Book Ten of the *Confessions* of Augustine (354–430). By *memoria* Augustine does not mean the memory, in the sense normally attached to it today. It is not primarily the recollection of past events but the 'deepest abyss of the ego', to use Henry Chadwick's phrase;[44] it is, in the words of John Burnaby, 'that deep of the soul in which is treasured not only the consciousness of the self, but a consciousness of God'.[45] It is *aula ingens*, 'a vast courtyard', a 'profound and infinite multiplicity', 'a large and boundless interiority' (*penetrale*). Within our *memoria* each of us finds contained 'the heaven, the earth, the sea': there we encounter our own true self, and not only ourselves but God.[46] The *memoria* is closely associated with the intellect (*mens*) and the spirit (*spiritus*). Our sense of identity and continuity is rooted in the memory; it is through the memory that we experience ourselves as created in God's image, and so become responsive to divine grace. There are manifest parallels here with the Biblical and Greek Patristic notion of the heart.

If the Greek Christian understanding of the heart resembles Augustine's *memoria*, it also anticipates the concept of the self as found in C. G. Jung. The self, as interpreted by Jung, signifies the totality of the human person. It denotes, not our ego-consciousness as apprehended at any specific moment, but the innermost depths of our personhood. In Jung's words, 'The self is not only the centre but the whole circumference which embraces both consciousness and unconscious; it is the centre of this totality, just as the ego is the centre of the conscious mind. . . . The self is our life's goal, for it is the completest expression of that fateful combination we call individuality.'[47] While there is no exact correspondence – in particular Jung places far greater emphasis on the unconscious than the Greek Fathers would have done – there is much in Jung that recalls what the Macarian *Homilies* say about the heart. Both are speaking about a unifying centre within us, a centre which includes all our conscious thoughts, our emotions and our will, but which exists at the same time on a deeper level that is primary and decisive.

In summary, then, it may be said that in Greek Patristic usage the notions of the heart and the soul overlap. Both terms refer to the same basic reality, but they approach this reality from somewhat different perspectives. This difference in perspective is apparent chiefly in two ways. First, the soul is normally seen as non-material, and is therefore contrasted with the body; the heart, on the other hand, is both a physical organ and a centre of spiritual energy, and so it symbolizes the fundamental unity of the human person. Second, while the word 'soul' has predominantly philosophical associations, the 'heart' is more explicitly religious in its overtones, indicating as it does the human person viewed as a spiritual subject, oriented towards God. Such are the two chief implications of the word heart, as compared with the soul: the heart designates the human being as a psychosomatic whole, and it designates the human being as a creature made in God's image, a finite expression of God's infinite self-expression.

Emotions and spiritual insight

How far does the notion of the soul extend? Is it more or less coterminous with the reason, or does it extend more broadly both downwards and upwards: downwards, so as to include the emotions or passions (there is unfortunately no English word that corresponds at all exactly to the Greek term *pathos*); and upwards, so as to include a faculty of spiritual vision and insight that is higher than the discursive reason?

There are indeed a number of Greek Christian writers who adopt a wide-ranging view of the soul, both downwards and upwards. First, as regards the emotions or passions, much depends upon the way in which the term *pathos* is understood. In this respect there exists among Patristic authors the same variation in standpoint as there is within Classical Greek philosophy. Many of the Fathers follow the Stoic approach, and see *pathos* in negative terms as something unnatural, excessive and disordered, that is to say, as a disease of the soul, that is not part of its true nature and that needs to be eliminated through *apatheia* ('dispassion', 'passionlessness'). This leads Clement of Alexandria to state that the truly good person has no passions.[48] Evagrius of Pontus (d.399), highly influential in the tradition of Greek ascetic theology, likewise adopts a sombre estimate of the passions, associating them with the demons. On this view, then, the passions are excluded from the soul.

Other Greek Fathers, however, prefer a more qualified approach, following Plato and Aristotle rather than the Stoics. According to this second group, which includes Theodoret of Cyrus (*c.*393–460) and Abba Isaias (d.489), as well as the Dionysian writings and Maximus the Confessor (*c.*580–662),[49] the passions are in themselves neither good nor bad but neutral; they only become virtuous or evil according to the use that we make of them. Thus, when members of this second group use the term *apatheia*, it means not the elimination of the passions but their purification. Our aim in regard to the passions, states Palamas, is not *nekrōsis*, their 'mortification', but rather *metathesis*, their 'transposition' or 'redirection'.[50] Desire (*epithymia*), says Maximus, is to be turned into *eros*, intense longing for God; wrath (*thymos*) is to become *agapē*, unselfish love.[51] On this second view, then, the passions are not in themselves parasitic distortions but have a place in the true nature of the soul.

Is this merely a linguistic point, a question of the way in which we choose to employ the word *pathos?* Surely more than this is at stake. It makes an enormous difference whether, when speaking to others or to ourselves, we say 'Suppress' or 'Transfigure', 'Destroy' or 'Reorient', 'Eliminate' or 'Educate'. This is a crucial point in all pastoral counselling.

If, then, the soul can extend downwards to include the passions or emotions, can it also extend upwards, to include some faculty of spiritual understanding superior to the power of ratiocination? Again, as with *pathos*, much depends on the way in which we choose to use words. Some Greek Christian writers, although by no means all, follow Plato in making a distinction between 'thinking' (*dianoia*), in the sense of reasoning from premisses to a conclusion, and intellect or 'intellection' (*nous*, *noēsis*).[52] When such a distinction is employed, 'intellection' means, not simply discursive thinking through the use of logical argumentation, but an intuitive, unmediated apprehension of eternal truth by means of inner vision. Through the *nous*, truth is simply 'seen' to be true; the *nous* is in this sense the 'eye' of the soul.[53] *Dianoia* is marked by plurality, whereas *noēsis* is unified, so that at its higher levels the subject–object dichotomy vanishes; in T. S. Eliot's phrase, 'You are the music while the music lasts.' Through *dianoia* we know about God; through *nous* we know God.

Dianoia, that is to say, forms general concepts by a process of abstraction from the data of sense-perception, and by manipulating these concepts it then argues to a conclusion through the use of classification and analysis. At this level of discursive reasoning the mind is deriving its information from material that is outside itself. On the level of *nous*, on the other hand, we participate directly in the reality that we contemplate. As Maximus observes, 'The [direct] experience (*peira*) of a thing suppresses the concept (*logos*) which represents that thing.' In this way we do not just argue or specu-late about the thing but we ourselves enter into it – or else it enters into us – so that our knowledge ceases to be multiform and becomes 'simple and integrated'.[54]

It is often affirmed that language is the essence of the human mind. My impression is that Maximus, and those Greek Christian writers who adopt an approach similar to his, would readily agree that this is true of the *dianoia*, but they would be more hesitant to say such a thing about the *nous*. On the contrary, intellection – at any rate on the higher levels of its activity – reaches out beyond language, visual images and mental concepts, and includes what today is commonly designated 'mystical experience', provided that we mean by this term, not levitation, telepathy, trances or other such paranormal phenomena, but the direct awareness of supra-natural reality. Maximus and his *confrères* would add that we are never more authentically human than when, through this exercise of *noēsis*, we transcend ourselves and enter into communion with the Eternal. In this sense, *nous* as our highest and most God-like faculty expresses our own true self.

From all this it will be evident that the imagination (*phantasia*) – understood by the Greek Fathers as the image-forming faculty dependent on sense-perception – stands on a level far below *noēsis*.

It is significant that almost all the references to *phantasia* in Lampe's *Patristic Greek Lexicon* carry a pejorative sense. One writer far too late to be included in Lampe, Nikodimos of the Holy Mountain (1748–1809), states that 'the devil has a very close relationship and familiarity with the imagination', and he goes so far as to style the *phantasia* 'a bridge of the devils'.[55] Coleridge's notion of the 'primary' imagination, however, corresponds not to the *phantasia*, as understood by the Greek Fathers, but much more closely to what they mean by *noēsis*.

What about the animals?

If the notion of the soul can be extended so as to include not only the rational aspect of human beings but also their emotions and affections, can it perhaps be enlarged still further so as to include the animals? Do they also have a soul? And if they do have a soul, is this soul the same in nature as the human soul?

Certainly, there is no lack of texts in the Greek Christian tradition which suggest that animals do indeed have souls, at any rate in some sense of the word. In the *Euchologion* or 'Book of Prayers', for example, used officially in the contemporary Greek Orthodox Church, there are several prayers for animals. One of these includes the words:

> Lord Jesus Christ, moved by your own tender mercy, pity the suffering animals. . . . For if a righteous man shows pity to the souls of his animals (cf. Prov. 12: 10), how should you not take pity on them, for you created them and you provide for them? In your compassion you did not forget the animals in the ark. . . . Through the good health and the plentiful number of oxen and other four-footed creatures, the earth is cultivated and its fruits increase; and your servants, who call upon your name, enjoy in full abundance the products of their farming.[56]

Origen argues at some length that animals have souls, stating categorically: 'No one, I suppose, will doubt that all living creatures whatever, even those that live in water, have souls.' He goes on to quote Scripture in support of this view (Gen. 1: 21, 24 [LXX]; Lev. 17: 14 [LXX]).[57]

But is this animal soul the same in nature as the human soul? Origen is prepared to acknowledge that there are similarities. Although in Greek it is usual to call animals 'irrational' (*aloga*),

Origen points out that many of them display something closely similar to human rationality: 'The instinct (*physis*) in hunting dogs and in war horses comes near, if I may say so, to reason itself.'[58] Here he is thinking only of domesticated animals; but Theophilus of Antioch (*c.*180) goes further, pointing out that the instinct in all animals, wild as well as domestic, which leads them to mate and to care for their offspring shows that they possess 'understanding'.[59] Other Greek Fathers maintain that animals share with humans, not only a certain degree of reason and understanding, but also memory and a wide range of emotions and affections. They display feelings of joy and grief, says Basil of Caesarea, and they recognize those whom they have met previously.[60] John Climacus adds that they express love for each other, for 'they often bewail the loss of their companions'.[61] We might add, recalling the story of Balaam's ass in Numbers 22: 22–34, that animals also possess spiritual vision, sometimes perceiving things to which we humans are blind.[62]

If all this is true, how far are we justified in making a sharp line of demarcation between animals and human beings? Surely Nemesius of Emesa is right to affirm that all living things – plants, animals and human beings – share together the same vital energy (*zoē*); creation as a whole constitutes a single unity.[63]

At the same time, however, the Greek Christian tradition believed that there is a crucial difference between animals and humans. Origen, basing himself on the creation account in Genesis 1, states what this is: the human soul is made in the divine image, while the animal soul is not.[64] This means that animals lack the conscious relationship with God that human beings enjoy, and so their souls are not endowed with immortality. The animal soul, according to Basil, is formed from the earth, and after death it is dissolved into the earth again;[65] human beings, on the other hand, possess 'the breath of life' breathed into them directly by God himself (Gen. 2: 7), and this enables them to attain the realm of eternity. C. S. Lewis, in his discussion of animal pain, suggests that perhaps we humans impart to the animals – at any rate to those that are tame – the immortality which in themselves they lack.[66] Unfortunately I can find no support for such a view in the Greek Fathers. They believed that there would be animals in the age to come, but they did not expect them to be precisely the same particular and individual animals existing at present. Individual human beings, in all their personal distinctness, will rise from the dead, but this will not happen with the animals. Presumably the animals in the end time will be, considered as particular individuals, *new* animals.

Was Greek Christianity justified in denying immortality to animals? Christ says that not a single sparrow is 'forgotten in God's sight'; God is concerned about the death of each one of them (Luke 12: 6; Matt. 10: 29). Christ does not say that sparrows have immortal life, but he does not deny the possibility. If the New Testament leaves the question open, should not we?

What Christ does say is that human persons are 'of more value than many sparrows' (Luke 12: 7; Matt. 10: 31). This is a point which Greek Christian writers take up and develop. They believe in a hierarchical universe, in which humans – by virtue of their creation in the divine image – have 'dominion' over the animals (Gen. 1: 27–8). Dominion, however, does not signify arbitrary domination or cruel exploitation, even though that is exactly the way in which it has been interpreted by many Christians through the ages. On the contrary, the dominion that is entrusted to us humans is precisely dominion according to the image and likeness of God; and so, in our exercise of this responsibility, we are to reflect the loving kindness and compassion of God. Such power as we have is to be exercised solely in obedience to God.[67]

Greek Christianity believes that there was once a time when, according to the paradise story, Adam and Eve lived at peace with the animals in the garden of Eden. It was human sin – our 'fall' into disobedience – that destroyed this harmony. But in the eschatological kingdom at the end time the primal harmony will be restored: 'The wolf shall live with the lamb, the leopard shall lie down with the kid . . . and a little child shall lead them' (Isa. 11: 6). In paradise humans, and also the animals, ate only plants (Gen. 1: 29–30); and presumably this will also be the case in the eschatological kingdom (in so far as the consumption of food still continues on that level of reality). Meat-eating was allowed to humankind by God only after the fall (Gen. 9: 3); it is therefore not in itself sinful, but at the same time it represents a decline from the original perfection. Thus the Orthodox Church has never been vegetarian as a matter of principle, even though monks and nuns usually abstain from meat. They eat fish, however, just as Christ himself did (Luke 24: 42–3).

The fact, then, that animals are considered in the Greek Christian tradition to lack an immortal soul formed according to the divine image does not mean that they are simply to be treated as objects undeserving of respect. On the contrary, the lives of the Greek saints – like those of their Western counterparts (especially Celtic) – abound in stories, often well authenticated, of close fellowship between beasts and humans. Such stories, so far from being whimsical or sentimental, are making a theological point: this mutual understanding between human beings and animals recalls the situation at the beginning in paradise, and it points forward to the transfigured cosmos that will be revealed in the end time. In the words of Isaac of Nineveh, honoured in the Greek tradition as Isaac the Syrian (seventh century),

> The humble man approaches the wild animals, and the moment they catch sight of him their ferocity is tamed. They come up and cling to him as to their master, wagging their tails and licking his hands and feet. For they smell on him the same smell that came from Adam before the transgression.[68]

Elsewhere Isaac writes in memorable terms about the compassion that we should show to animals:

> What is a merciful heart? . . . It is a heart on fire for the whole of creation, for humanity, for the birds, for the animals, for the demons, and for all that exists. . . . As a result of his deep mercy the heart of such a person shrinks and cannot bear to hear or to look on any injury or the slightest suffering of anything in creation. That is why he constantly offers up prayer full of tears even for the irrational animals. . . . He even prays for the reptiles as a result of the great compassion that is poured out beyond measure in is heart, after the likeness of God.[69]

A twentieth-century Orthodox saint, the Russian monk Silouan the Athonite (1866–1938), expresses the same intensity of compassion:

> The Lord bestows such rich grace on his chosen that they embrace the whole earth, the whole world, with their love. . . . One day . . . I saw a dead snake on my path which had been chopped in pieces, and each piece writhed convulsively, and I was filled with pity for every living creature, every suffering thing in creation, and I wept bitterly before God.[70]

In practice Eastern Christendom may not always have behaved with the generosity of spirit displayed by Isaac and Silouan, but such at any rate is its aim and hope.

Within the understanding of the soul upheld by Greek Christianity, what in conclusion are the elements that we today might find helpful and illuminating? For myself I would answer by singling out two themes. First, there is the notion of the heart as the unifying centre of our personhood, open on the side to the abyss of our unconscious, open on the other to the abyss of divine grace. Second, there is the understanding of the *nous* or intellect as a faculty far higher than the reasoning brain – a visionary power, creative and self-transcending, that reaches out beyond time into eternity, beyond words into silence.

Notes

1 *The Pedagogue* 3.1.1; cf. 1 John 3: 2.
2 *Catechesis* 6. 6.
3 *On the incomprehensibility of God* 5 (ed. Malingrey, 259–60).
4 *Modern Man in Search of a Soul* (London, 1984), 86.
5 *On the creation of man* 11 (*PG* (= *Patrologia Graeca*) 44. 156AB).
6 *Apology for Origen* 8 (*PG* 17.604A).
7 *Of the nature of man* 2 (ed. Morani, 16.12).
8 *On the soul and the resurrection* (*PG* 46.29AB).
9 *Questions to Antiochus* 16 (*PG* 28.608A).
10 The phrase is Pauline: Rom. 7: 22; 2 Cor. 4: 16; Eph. 3: 16.
11 *Spiritual Homilies* (Collection II or H) 7. 8.
12 *Panarion* 70.3.1; *Ancoratus* 55.4–5.
13 *Against the heresies* 5.6.1.
14 See Antoine Guillaumont, *Les 'Kephalaia Gnostica' d'Évagre le Pontique et l'histoire de l'Origénisme chez les Grecs et chez les Syriens* (Patristica Sorbonensia 5: Paris, 1962), 144, where further references are given.
15 *Spiritual Homilies* 15.10; cf. Luke 21: 18.
16 *On the creation of man* 27 (*PG* 44.225C–228A); compare *On the soul and the resurrection* (*PG* 46.73A–80A, 145B–148A); *On the dead* (*PG* 46.532B–536B; ed. Jaeger/Heil, 62–6).
17 C. S. Lewis, *Miracles: A Preliminary Study* (London, 1947), 180. Gregory of Nyssa uses similar analogies in *On the soul and the resurrection* (*PG* 46.141AB: a stream, the flame of a candle).
18 Plato (?), *First Alcibiades* 130c.
19 *In I Cor.c.15, lect.* 2. (ed. Cai, §924).
20 For a very emphatic assertion of this viewpoint, see the work attributed to Justin Martyr (*c.*100–*c.*165) but probably spurious, *On the resurrection* 8 (*PG* 6.1585B).
21 Denzinger–Schönmetzer, *Enchiridion Symbolorum* (36th edn, revised: Barcelona, 1976), § 301.
22 *On first principles* 3. 4.1. For the phrase 'vital spirit' , see Wisdom 15.11. Gregory of Nyssa is also a trichotomist: see *On the creation of man* 8 (*PG* 44.145D).
23 *Commentary on John* 32. 18 (ed. Preuschen, 455.17–18).

24 See R. A. Norris, *Manhood and Christ. A Study in the Christology of Theodore of Mopsuestia* (Oxford, 1963), 81–122.
25 See the useful discussion in D. S. Wallace-Hadrill, *The Greek Patristic View of Nature* (Manchester, 1968), esp. 65–75.
26 Compare Henry Chadwick, 'Origen, Celsus, and the Resurrection of the Body', *Harvard Theological Review* 41 (1948), 83–102.
27 *Stromateis* 6.8 (ed. Stählin, 466.13–14).
28 *Homily* 3.7 (*PG* 31.213C; ed. Rudberg, 35.6–7).
29 *Republic* 4 (434d–441c).
30 See Clement of Alexandria, *The Pedagogue* 3.1.2; Gregory of Nazianzus, *Poems* 2.1.47 (*PG* 37.1381A–1384A); Evagrius, *Practicus* 89 (ed. Guillaumont, 680–2).
31 *On first principles* 3.4.1.
32 *On the soul* 2 (413b11–13).
33 *On the creation of man* 8 (*PG* 44.144D–145A).
34 *On the creation of man* 15 (*PG* 44.176B–177A).
35 See e.g. *Republic* 10 (611b).
36 For the Patristic understanding of the heart, the best discussion is still that of Antoine Guillaumont: see his articles 'Les sens des noms du coeur dans l'antiquité', *Le coeur* (Études Carmélitaines 29: Paris, 1950), pp. 41–81; 'Le "coeur" chez les spirituels grecs à l'époque ancienne', *Dictionnaire de spiritualité* 2 (1952), cols 2281–8.
37 *Pensées* (ed. Brunschvicg) 4.277.
38 See e.g. Matt. 6: 21, 15: 19; Luke 2: 19; Rom. 1: 24, 8: 27; Gal. 4: 6; Eph. 3: 16–17.
39 *Spiritual Homilies* 15.20; cf. 15.22–33; 43.7
40 Ibid. 15.32. Cf. Ps. 63 [64]: 7 (LXX): 'The heart is deep.'
41 *Triads in defence of the Holy Hesychasts* 1.2.3–4, quoting John Climacus, *The Ladder of Divine Ascent* 26 (*PG* 88.1020A), and Macarius, *Spiritual Homilies* 15.20.
42 *Triads* 1.2.8. On the psychosomatic technique of the Hesychasts, see Kallistos Ware, 'Praying with the body: the hesychast method and non-Christian parallels', *Sobornost incorporating Eastern Churches Review* 14:2 (1992), 6–35.
43 The phrase, borrowed from Vladimir Lossky, is used by Jacques-Albert Cuttat, *The Encounter of Religions: A dialogue between the West and the Orient, with an Essay on the Prayer of Jesus* (New York and Tournai, 1960), 92–3.
44 *Augustine* (Oxford and New York, 1986), 67.
45 *Amor Dei: A Study of the Religion of St Augustine* (London, 1938), 155. Compare Aimé Solignac, ' "Memoria" dans la tradition augustinienne', *Dictionnaire de spiritualité* 10 (1978), cols 994–1002.
46 Augustine, *Confessions* 10.8.14–15; 10.17.26.
47 *Memories, Dreams, Reflections*, ed. Aniela Jaffé (London, 1967), 417.
48 *Stromateis* 7.11 (ed. Stählin, 47.1).
49 For detailed references, see Kallistos Ware, 'The meaning of "Pathos" in Abba Isaias and Theodoret of Cyrus' , in Elizabeth A. Livingstone (ed.), *Studia Patristica* 20 (Leuven, 1989), 315–22.
50 *Triads* 3.3.15.
51 *On love* 2.48.

52 *Republic* 6 (509d–511e).
53 The *nous* is so described in Macarius, *Spiritual Homilies* 7.8.
54 *To Thalassius, question* 60 (*PG* 90.624A; ed. Laga and Steel, 77).
55 *A Handbook of Spiritual Counsel*, trans. Peter A. Chamberas (The Classics of Western Spirituality: New York and Mahwah, 1989), 149, 151. He sees the imagination as specifically an attribute of fallen humankind; while still in Paradise, Adam had no *phantasia*.
56 'Prayer of St Modestos', *Mikron Euchologion i Hagiasmatarion* (Apostoliki Diakonia: Athens, 1984), 297. The prayer is attributed to Nikodimos of the Holy Mountain.
57 *On first principles* 2.8.1
58 Ibid. 3.1.3.
59 To *Autolycus* 1.6.
60 *Hexaemeron* 8.1 (*PG* 29.165AB).
61 *Ladder of Divine Ascent* 26 (*PG* 88.1028A).
62 Compare the view of the Italian G.-P. Monti (1713–83), who was willing to ascribe to animals a genuine spiritual life, although only on a rudimentary level: see E. Amann, in *Dictionnaire de théologie catholique* 10: 2 (1929), col. 2394.
63 *Of the nature of man* 1 (ed. Morani, 2.13–14, 3.3–25).
64 *Against Celsus* 4.83.
65 *Hexaemeron* 8.2 (PG 29.168A).
66 *The Problem of Pain* (London, 1940), 124–31. Duns Scotus (*c.*1265–1308) seems also to have entertained the possibility that animals may share in the resurrection of the dead: see P. Raymond, in *Dictionnaire de théologie catholique* 4: 2 (1924), col. 1933.
67 Note the respect for animals shown in the Jewish tradition: Robert Murray, *The Cosmic Covenant* (London, 1992), 94–125.
68 *Homily* 82, in *Mystic Treatises by Isaac of Nineveh*, trans. A. J. Wensinck (Amsterdam, 1923), 386.
69 *Homily* 74, ibid. 341.
70 Archimandrite Sophrony (Sakharov), *Saint Silouan the Athonite* (Tolleshunt Knights, 1991), 367, 469.

References

Ellverson, A.-S., *The Dual Nature of Man: A Study in the Theological Anthropology of Gregory of Nazianzus* (Uppsala, 1981).
Ladner, G. B., 'The Philosophical Anthropology of Saint Gregory of Nyssa', *Dumbarton Oaks Papers* 12 (1958), 61–94.
Linzey, A., *Animal Theology* (London, 1994).
Nellas, P., *Deification in Christ: Orthodox Perspectives on the Nature of the Human Person* (Crestwood, 1987).
Stead, C. G., *The Changing Self. A Study on the Soul in Later Neoplatonism* (Brussels, 1978).
Thunberg, L., *Microcosm and Mediator. The Theological Anthropology of Maximus the Confessor* (2nd edn: Chicago and La Salle, 1995).
Wallace-Hadrill, D. S., *The Greek Patristic View of Nature* (Manchester, 1968).

Ware, Kallistos, 'The Unity of the Human Person according to the Greek Fathers', in A. Peacocke and G. Gillett (eds.), *Persons and Personality: A Contemporary Inquiry* (Oxford, 1987), 197–206.

—— 'The Meaning of "Pathos" in Abba Isaias and Theodoret of Cyrus', *Studia Patristica* 20 (Leuven, 1989), 315–22.

—— ' "In the Image and Likeness": The Uniqueness of the Human Person', in J. T. Chirban (ed.), *Personhood: Orthodox Christianity and the Connection between Body, Mind and Soul* (Westport and London, 1996), 1–13.

5

SHAMANISM AND THE
UNCONFINED SOUL

Peter Rivière

The three previous contributors to this volume have been concerned
with the same tradition; one that is both literate and historical. This
chapter makes a radical break with what has gone before. The material on which it relies belongs neither to a literate nor an historical
tradition in the sense that there is a continuity of debate. Rather the
material on which it is based is orally received and visually observed.
Furthermore native exegesis and practice come filtered through an
alien medium, the ethnographer, and distorted through translation
into concepts that do not easily fit with the native notions. The act of
translation, necessarily into terms with which we are acquainted, has
the tendency to make the exotic more familiar than perhaps it is.
Thus many of the English terms that appear in earlier chapters will
crop up again but this does not mean that a Greek Christian, for
example, and an Amerindian are talking about the same thing. The
alternative would be to use the native terms, but I think this would
be too demanding given that I am going to use a range of examples
from a number of different languages. Accordingly, I have avoided as
far as possible the use of vernacular terms. It might be added here that
there is also the opposite problem; the idioms in which certain ideas
are expressed often make similarities difficult to recognize.

    With the exception of a brief reference to the transmigration of
the shamans' souls among ancient Greeks, the three previous contributors seem to have taken as an implicit assumption that the soul
is securely conjoined with its owner or body, at least until death.
Here that assumption has to be abandoned because it is almost a
given of shamanism and in the cultures where the practice is found
that the soul, or at least one soul where there is more than one, is
a relatively mobile, even free, agent.

As with so many widespread practices and institutions, a definition of shamanism that will embrace the phenomenon in all its multiple cross-cultural guises has been difficult to agree. Indeed anthropology has mainly given up the sterile task of definition, and is happy to use shamanism, as it does with many other terms, simply as a signpost, pointing in a general direction rather than to a single destination. This allows us to know approximately what area we are in but leaves the exact charting of the phenomenon to be locally ascertained.

Even so, and with that caveat, in a volume such as this, some of whose readers may be unfamiliar with shamanism and what it entails, I should offer a few introductory remarks about the nature of shamanism before plunging into detail. The classic work on the subject is that by Mircea Eliade (1964), devoted mainly to Siberian material, including that from the Tungus, from whose language the word is derived. For Eliade, shamanism is above all a technique of ecstasy by means of which shamans' souls are able to leave their bodies and travel to different levels of the cosmos. Another important feature for Eliade is the shamans' special relationship with their familiars or spirit-helpers. The essential thing, and that which distinguishes shamanism from spirit possession, is that shamans take an active role in their relation with spirits, controlling them rather than being simply possessed by them. These two central features are also to be found in the shamanic ideas of the native peoples of Tropical Forest South America. This region is going to be the main focus of my attention for the simple reason that it is the ethnographic area I know best and on which I can claim, if not expertise, at least some first-hand experience. Furthermore it is a region in which shamanism is still intensively and extensively practised. It is well documented that contact, far from eliminating the practice, has often increased its incidence. I will not be dealing with all aspects of South American shamanism; indeed, given the complexity of the phenomenon this would not be possible in the space available. Rather, because of the focus of this book, I will look at the shaman as a specialist in souls, a soul minder. In his role as such (and I say 'his' advisedly as there are relatively few recorded cases of female shamans in the region), the shaman provides an excellent entrée to the notions of the soul in Lowland South America. I shall begin by talking about South American shamanism, the cosmologies within which it operates, and then turn to the question of the soul.

The shamanic ideas and practices of the native peoples of Tropical Forest South America vary in some degree from the classic form found in Siberia – we do not need to discuss these differences in detail but let me give you an obvious example. For Eliade, classic shamanism involved the spontaneous achievement of ecstasy, and the use of drugs to achieve it he regarded as an impoverished form. Shamanism in South America, especially within the tropical forest, is very much concerned with the sophisticated use of a whole range of narcotic and hallucinogenic substances in order to obtain a trance state. The word 'sophisticated' should be stressed since there is a deep knowledge and understanding of the varying affects of different substances, taken in different strengths, in different conditions and under different circumstances.

There is variation across the tropical forest, both in the use of hallucinogenic and narcotic substances and in other practices, ideas and accoutrements. In general terms, however, the main features of Lowland South American shamanism are the ability of the shaman to visit other cosmic levels, to enter into a relationship either with the spirit world generally or with individual members of the spirit world who act as his assistants. But above all the shaman must be able to see. This is nicely encapsulated in the title of what is perhaps one of the best books on Amazonian shamanism, Jean-Pierre Chaumeil's *Voir, savoir, pouvoir*. To see is to know is to be able, in other words, to have power. It should be added that for the Amerindian power tends to be an ambivalent quality. The power to cure is also the power to kill; accordingly shamans as well as being curers are killers. The basic principle being: our shaman good, your shaman bad. This, in turns, fits with a wider view of the ambivalent nature of the spirit world.

But what is meant by 'see' in this context? To explain that I need to give a brief description of Amerindian cosmology. The basic Amerindian cosmos, although often highly elaborated, consists of three levels; the sky, the earth and a watery underworld. Whereas ordinary people in this life are mainly confined to the earthly layer, shamans are able to visit the other layers, or at least their souls are. The layers are inhabited by a range of non-human entities – some of them animals but also spirits and monsters. A further important feature of the world is that the visible world has an invisible counterpart, in some ways more real than this world. It is that other world which a person, to be a shaman, must have the sight to see. It is in that invisible world that the causes and explanations of the apparently contingent events in the visible world are to be found. This is not as absurd as one might think and to some extent it is the idiom in which such theories are expressed that make them seem so alien to us. We might remember that while we may feel and discern the symptoms of a disease, the causes – germs, microbes, viruses or whatever – can only be identified, perhaps seen, by specialists using the right procedures and instruments.

The degree to which lay people have access to the invisible world varies greatly. In some groups virtually no one, other than a shaman, has this ability, and an uncontrolled or unintentional sighting of a being from the counterpart world is regarded as a dangerous omen. At the other extreme, virtually every member of the society has some contact with the invisible and real world, usually achieved by the use of an hallucinogenic substance. These experiences are often regarded as an essential part of education; a way of learning about how the world works and thus how to operate in it. There is even a recorded case of a people who give hallucinogens to hunting dogs in order to enhance their performance (Harner 1972: 63). This does not mean that these sightings of the other world are fully comprehensible to lay people who instead rely on the commentaries of the specialist shaman to interpret their hallucinogenically induced experiences. In other words, lay people tend to have a passive relationship with the other world compared with the shaman's active involvement with it. Shamanic ability is not necessarily an all or nothing quality, but the degree of competence in dealing with a shamanic world-view.

There is another related matter that also needs some explanation. The Amerindian lives in a highly transformational world. Gertrude Stein's view on roses just does not apply in the tropical forest. External appearances are not to be trusted; things are not necessarily what they appear to be. This is often expressed in terms of clothes (cf. Rivière 1995). In other words, the wild pig you meet in the forest may be just that, but it may be a spirit wearing wild pig clothes. The outcome of the encounter may well give a clue to the reality. Thus a hunter may use as an excuse – but not too often – that the wild pig he shot just disappeared and thus was in reality a spirit. Shamans and the characters in many Amerindian myths also exhibit this unstable quality and remain undefined as human, animal or spirit. Appearances are deceiving and reality lies behind them. Another aspect of this is that the large majority of supernatural beings are neither good nor bad in any absolute sense but may turn out to be either one or the other, depending on the outcome of an encounter. Now the shaman, through his power of sight, is able to see through the outer covering, the clothing, to identify instantaneously the true nature of the creature. The use of those words 'true nature' is where the difficulties really begin.

We have seen that the shaman is able, normally in a trance, to detach his soul to visit the other layers of the cosmos and see into the invisible world in order to discover the genuine reasons for events in this world. He is a specialist in the invisible where the true nature of things lies. At this point, we turn to the 'soul'. I am going to use the word 'soul', because that is what this volume is about. I also think there is no danger of my being misunderstood and of anyone assuming that I am referring to some specific and identifiable entity – the sheer vagueness and uncertainty that surrounds our own use of the concept ensures that. There are a number of other words that one might choose to use and have been variously used by writers on the region. These include essence (which would be my own choice), life, life-force, will, consciousness and in the case of one ethnographer 'interactive self'. However, whatever term an ethnographer has chosen, it should be remembered that the term will reflect a dialectical relationship between what word is available in English or other European language in which to express the notion and the particular emphasis in its indigenous usage. In each case the use of the single word is an inadequate translation for what are extremely complex notions, and many ethnographers have preferred to provide a gloss and then stick with the vernacular terms.

For the present purpose we may note that all Amerindian groups recognize a concept for which we are using the shorthand, 'soul'. Furthermore virtually everything in the world is normally seen as endowed with a soul, an invisible essential aspect. It has been said that one of the paradoxical results of the evangelization of Amerindians is their secularization because their own lives are far more spiritual than those of the Christian missionaries attempting to convert them. The latter accept physical causation more readily than the Amerindian.

Perhaps this is the right place to point out that until prodded into it by the ethnographer there is often little indigenous inclination to intellectualize the soul or systematize ideas about it. Rather it is a lived experience. This is a crucial difference from the theologians and philosophers dealt with in earlier chapters because the South American specialist tends to be a practitioner at least as much as a thinker. I cannot help wondering what the daily, practical implications were for Aquinas of the ideas he had about the soul. The South American specialists have hands-on experience; something that few European philosophers and theologians would claim.

The traditional term for this set of ideas whereby much of nature is endowed with spirit or soul is animism, but it is one which today is used with caution if at all. The reason for this is summarized well by the French anthropologist Philippe Descola. I quote:

> Among other things, animism is the belief that natural beings possess their own spiritual principles and that it is therefore possible for humans to establish with these entities personal relations of a certain kind – relations of protection, seduction, hostility, alliance, or exchange of services. Modern anthropology has been extremely reticent on the topic of animism thus defined, perhaps out of an implicit fear of drawing undue attention to an apparently irrational aspect of the life of archaic societies – an aspect that cannot easily be reduced to one of those universal operations of the mind which have been identified as the 'logic of the concrete' and which can be shown to operate in myths or taxonomies. (1992: 114)

Descola goes on to suggest that we should recognize animic systems, which are the symmetrical inversion of totemic systems. In animic systems nature and supernature are socialized – plants and animals are treated as proper persons. According to group, there is a varying degree of intercourse between humans and these other 'proper persons', but everywhere it is the shaman who has privileged access to and communication with them. The tropical forests of Lowland South America abound in such systems. Everywhere one finds the idea that every animate being, and what constitutes the category of 'animate being' needs to be discovered case by case, has a soul or, at least, partakes of the soul of its original being. However, it is important to point out that it is only the souls of relatively few animate beings that are regarded as significant and impinge on human affairs. At the same time if lists of such beings drawn up from different parts of the region show some variation, the same creatures and plants figure on them again and again. So while it is necessary to remember that these animic systems provide the context, I shall now turn to deal mainly with the human soul although it may not be regarded as conceptually or qualitively different from that of other animate beings.

The literature from Lowland South America dealing with the soul is vast and, as one might imagine, the information obtained on the subject varies greatly, not only between groups but also between informants within the same group. This should occasion no surprise as there were likewise disagreements among the European commentators on the nature of the soul. As Bishop Ware remarks there was, in Greek Christian thought, no single doctrine about the soul, but a wide variety of approaches to what in the end is a mystery. Even so the protagonists in those arguments, contemporary with one another or not, operated within a recognizable tradition. They were aware of the terms of the debate. This, of course, is not true in South America where shamans do not meet at conferences or in schools to systematize their ideas on the soul and argue about them. At the same time, one cannot fail to notice how often similar ideas about the soul recur among the native peoples of Lowland South America.

How far does this make it safe to generalize about notions of the soul in the region? One of the few to attempt it is Lawrence Sullivan. In his magisterial survey of South American religions, *Icanchu's Drum*, he has tried to synthesize the South American ideas on the soul. In particular he identifies a difference between two kinds of soul; one that exhibits physiological and the other epistemological tendencies (1988: 248–9). The clearest example of this that I am aware of is that of the Piaroa of Venezuela. The Piaroa distinguish a 'life of thought' from a 'life of the senses'. Whereas humans possess both these, gods have only the former and animals only the latter. However, young children, like animals, have only a life of senses, and formal education consists of the mastery of the senses by the knowledge that comes with the life of thought (Overing 1988). Sullivan, however, is aware that his identification of two types of soul is a desire for intellectual clarity and rational order that often fails to fit with the particular facts of the case. As he writes:

> The full range of the soul's experience should not be confused with the theoretical apparatus used to think about it since the soul's elements circumscribe the whole of spiritual existence and not simply rational inquiry. (1988: 249)

In other words some understanding of Amerindian souls is more likely to be achieved through specific examples rather than abstract generalizations. On this basis I wish to present to you some examples, inevitably in simplified form as you will have understood by now that the notion of soul pervades all aspects of the Amerindian's life. The cases have been chosen in order to illustrate both the variation and the similarity of the ideas and practices relating to the soul across the vast region of Lowland South America. I could have selected others, equally good and interesting, but even if I had I doubt that the final result, a set of themes combining in different ways to form a variety of pictures, would be very different. The analogy I would like to use, although like all analogies this one has its limitations, is the kaleidoscope. The same pieces in the kaleidoscope form different patterns as one moves it round. Thus, as one moves round the tropical forest, the same themes re-emerge but in different relations to one another, producing different pictures.

The first example comes from my research with the Carib-speaking Trio Indians who live astride the Surinam–Brazilian border. They are fairly typical slash-and-burn cultivators of the tropical forest. Among these people the person is composed of body (*pun*), soul (*amore*) and name (*eka*). The Trio subscribe to two world-wide ideas. The first, which I am not going to discuss further, is that the same word is used for soul and shadow; and the second is the close association between soul and name. I will return to this in a moment but here it might be noted that among many Carib-speakers, including neighbouring groups, the word for soul is similar to or cognate with the Trio term for name. They share the same root '*ka*'. The Trio soul can best be described as a morally neutral concept, something akin to our notion of consciousness in its sense of the totality of thoughts and feelings which constitute a person's conscious being. It is more than this in so far as there are degrees of consciousness that are associated with status, prowess and knowledge.

The soul is thought to permeate the body with special concentrations at the heart and pulses. Attempts to find out whether these are different aspects of a single soul or multiple souls produced a very variable response. However, and although the same word is used for it, there is the recognition of a distinct eye-soul that is extinguished on death. This fits with some other cases that I will turn to shortly in which the eye-soul is explicitly equated with what may be translated as 'life'.

It is said that babies receive their soul through the fontanelle at birth. The soul of the newborn child is small and not secured to the body and there is great danger that, unless the correct ritual procedures are observed by the parents, the soul will abandon the infant. The reason for this has to do with ideas of consubstantiality between parents and child. This idea is more general than that and consubstantiality is also thought to exist between husband and wife and in varying degrees among other kin. What is shared is soul or essence so that those with whom you are consubstantial are affected by your actions and you by theirs. In other words a person's essence is not entirely discrete. This should not be too difficult a notion for us to understand since our own idiom of kinship is often expressed in terms of shared blood, or more recently 'genetic make-up'. It might be noted that in some South American societies blood is seen as the physical and visible representation of the soul.

As the Trio child grows up the soul becomes increasingly fixed to the body, but never totally. The soul leaves the body during dreams and this is understood as normal. In fact the vernacular term for dreaming literally means 'to provide oneself with a soul'. What is not normal is when the soul is absent from the body under other conditions, above all during sickness. I do not have time to consider Trio aetiology in depth, but, as with most other people in the region, causes lie in the invisible world and it is there that one has to look to understand events in the visible world. They are the result of human activation of spirits or direct spirit intervention, or a combination of both. One diagnosis of sickness is soul-loss, and here the dividing line between sickness and death becomes blurred – the state of someone unconscious in a coma or dead is described by the same word, *wakenai*. This term literally translates as 'not being' and the answer to what is not being is the soul. It is not without interest that among the western neighbours of the Trio, the Waiwai, the word for an infant literally translates as 'little not being'. This reflects the perceived association between the states of infancy, sickness and death as they are all conditions under which the soul and body are in a tenuous relationship. Good health, on the other hand, is manifest in a secure, firm relationship between body and soul; the hardness of the person.

Among the Trio the shaman is the only person with access to the invisible world and it is accordingly his responsibility to deal with sickness which is presumed to originate there. There are various diagnoses possible – for example, the sickness may be caused by invisible spirit darts that have been shot into the patient and which the shaman attempts to remove. Where soul-loss has occurred, it may be the result of the soul just having wandered off of its own accord or it may have been captured by spirits. Either way, the shaman's task is to enter the invisible world and cross the cosmic layers in search of it and bring it back. In this he is helped by his familiars or spirit helpers. Shamanic journeys are not without danger and the shaman often has to engage in violent struggles with the hostile spirits in order to wrest the patient's soul from them and return it safely.

Death provides a privileged moment in which to understand the soul as it is when the person is, so to speak, unassembled. I will deal with the Trio's eschatological beliefs quite briefly. At death the mortal body is disposed of, traditionally buried in the floor of the house which is abandoned. The immortal soul departs on a hazardous journey through the sky to a soul reservoir on the eastern horizon. The descriptions I obtained of this place are less than clear, but it appears to be like a lake of soul matter. At death the soul gets poured back into the lake and becomes indistinguishable as an entity; just like pouring a cup of water into a bucket of water. At birth a cup of water is scooped out so that whereas any newborn may have a few particles of someone's former soul the odds of getting all of exactly the same particles are remote. In other words, although soul matter is recycled so that any particular soul is constituted of particles from former souls, in itself it will almost certainly be unique. Thus in terms of soul it is difficult to talk about reincarnation, but what does get reincarnated is that aspect of the individual signified by a name.

The name is the link between the body and the soul, or better perhaps the signifier of the joint presence of body and soul as a person in the visible world. Names are transmitted through alternate generations, a person receiving the name of a recently deceased member of the grandparental generation. The name on the death of its bearer goes into abeyance but it is under these circumstances that the significance of the name in the relationship between body and soul becomes fully apparent. In Trio to ask the name of a dead person makes no sense – in other words a question such as 'what is the name of your deceased father?' is not understood. The properly formulated question is 'what is the deceased name of your father?'. The Trio point out quite reasonably that just because your father is dead this does not mean that he has ceased to be your father. In other words, it is not the relationship that has ceased to exist but the name which signifies and binds together body and soul as a living, visible, social being. Finally, the root of the word for name is the same as that for the verb 'to be' or 'to speak'. Although I have had no chance to check with a Trio what they would make of it, I am fairly certain that the closest one could get in Trio to 'Cogito, ergo sum' is *Wïka, irëme wejae*, or 'I do or speak, therefore I am'.

In my next two cases, which I will treat more briefly, I want to take further the question of multiple souls. First let us look at the Yekuana of Southern Venezuela, another Carib-speaking group of tropical forest cultivators. The Yekuana recognize the existence of six souls although all of them involve verbal elaborations of a single basic term, *akato,* in which we may note once again the '*ka*' root. Two of them, the heart-soul and the eye-soul, are contained within the body, represent immortal life, and return to heaven on death. These souls are morally neutral in contrast with the other four which are external to the body. One of these, the 'soul in the sun', is the force of moral goodness and returns to the sun on death. The other three are concerned with moral wickedness. The 'soul in the moon' is the main receptacle for evil thoughts and actions and it suffers forever on the death of the person. Then there is the 'soul in the water', visible as the reflection in the water, which also helps absorb or redeem wickedness. Finally, the 'soul in the earth', or shadow, is an ambivalent entity that after death wanders the earth in the form of a small dwarf making bleating sounds (Guss 1989: 50–1). Although Yekuana ideas, especially in their moral aspect, are more elaborate than those of the Trio, or perhaps those of my informants, or perhaps blessed with a better ethnographer, they exhibit many similar principles.

My next case takes the topic one stage further. They are the Yagua of north-east Peru, another group of tropical forest cultivators whose language is probably of very distant Carib origin. Here it is a matter of five souls, each of which is known by a different word in the Yagua language. However bilingual Indians, that is to say speaking Yagua and Spanish, when using the latter, refer to two of them as spirits and the other three as souls. The two spirits are the animating force in the human body. One of these accounts for the movements and actions of the body and the term for it also means shadow. The second is concerned with intelligence and understanding and is an eye-soul. The spirits are immortal and at death go to the 'land of the dead'. A person's three souls come into existence only on death; they are malevolent and survive for only a limited period. The 'soul of the day' fulfils a similar function to the Yekuana 'soul in the moon' and is the redeemed wickedness of the deceased. The 'soul of the night' resides in the grave whence it comes forth at night seeking vengeance. The 'soul of the zenith' is the most dangerous of the three; it appears at midday and is responsible for spreading sickness. A powerful shaman is able to convert these souls into spirit helpers, whereas those of lesser competence are only able to conduct rites to keep them at bay (Chaumeil 1983: 91–6; 253).

The idea of souls that only come into existence following the death of the person is quite widespread through Lowland South America as is that about the degree of mortality and immortality of different types of soul. I will illustrate this by turning to the Barasana, a Tukanoan people of the Colombian Amazon. For the Barasana the person is composed of a body formed from soft and hard parts. The soft parts are exemplified by the heart, the container of blood, and the lungs, container of breath. The soft parts are seen as the female contribution to the person and the feminine mani-festation of the soul (*usu*). At the same time blood and breath are opposed as female and male. The main male contribution is semen from which the bones of a person are formed and which have a soul aspect. Alongside these bodily or material souls is a pure, non-material soul represented by the name. These souls, variously associated with heart, lungs, bones and names, are all referred to by the same term and are regarded as essential for life. However, there is a clear difference, which emerges at death, between the souls associated with bodily parts and the name soul. The former disap-pear as the body decays, so that the soul of the soft parts, the feminine aspect, perishes before that of the bones. The name soul, on the other hand, is immortal and returns to the ancestral house until called upon again (Hugh-Jones 1979: 133–5). The Barasana also recognize other 'soul' aspects of the person but I will leave those to one side as what I wish to stress in this example is the idea that hardness is associated with durability, but the hardest souls, the immortal ones, are represented by things, such as names, which are physically the most insubstantial. This is even more apparent in the next example.

These are the Bororo of Central Brazil who live to the south of the tropical forest region and in many social and cultural aspects are different from the previous examples. For my account of them I rely on the work of Christopher Crocker entitled *Vital souls*. The Bororo have two concepts central to the ordering of their world; in the vernacular they are *aroe* and *bope*, which may be crudely trans-lated as essence and process respectively. I will cite Crocker's words to define these concepts.

> Any category of physical thing has another modality of being, which they identify as *aroe*. This is an essence, or soul, or, sometimes, a name (33).

> [B]*ope* . . . are . . . the principle of all organic transforma-tion, of fructification, growth, death and decay, the spirit of metamorphoses. Hence they oppose and complement the *aroe*, the representatives of immutable categorical form (36).

81

Finally:

> The *bope* as generators of all transformations are fluid, evanescent creatures, forever oozing out of one form and into another. . . . All of this amorphousness contrasts with the *aroe*, which are literally the personification of timeless categories, unaltering forms of name and being (132).

While essence and process are opposed as the souls of immutable forms and spirits of changing substance, they also exist as an unstable synthesis in every living creature and much Bororo effort is devoted to the maintenance of balance within this synthesis. Everything in the universe belongs on a continuum ranging from total 'bopeness' to pure 'aroeness'. Towards the centre of this continuum lie human beings. In humans *aroe* is represented by an immortal name and a transcendent soul. *Bope* is present in the organic being and above all in *raka*.

Raka is another complex concept. The simple translation is blood and other organic fluids, but it is much more than that. It is energy, the life-force which animates everything. While it is intimately associated with the *bope*, the *aroe* soul's welfare also depends on the quantity of *raka* within the body. The manifestation of the former is blood, of the latter breath. Most Bororo health practices are concerned with the conservation of *raka*, and sickness and death are its temporary and permanent loss respectively. Even so humans cannot escape expending their *raka* through physical labour, copulation, singing and dancing; the older people are, inevitably the less *raka* they have. It is also the common substance that unites members of nuclear families. Thus *bope* and *raka* are intimately related as part of normal change and decay, but in order to keep this process, regarded as inevitable, 'normal' it has to be integrated with the timeless and immutable categories of *aroe*. It is a consequence of human failure to maintain the proper relationship between essence and process that is the cause of the chaos that constantly threatens the moral and natural order. The Bororo believe themselves to live in a naturally entropic world.

The persons responsible for repairing the damage when things get out of order are the shamans. The Bororo have two types of shaman. One who is responsible for dealing with the *aroe*, the other with the *bope*. These two types are contrasted in many different ways but for present purposes we may restrict ourselves to a limited number of aspects. The *bope* shaman's main routine task is the 'pasteurization', a sort of shamanic cooking, of certain foods that are strong in *raka* in order to make them edible for lay people. Their other main functions are predicting the future, treating the sick and protecting members of the village from attack by hostile *bope* who try to enter the village, usually at night to steal the *aroe* soul of sleeping persons. In these activities the shaman is helped by his own *bope* soul and his *bope* familiars. His work is mainly directed towards individuals and the temporal processes of life.

In contrast to this are the shamans of the *aroe*. The literal translation of the term by which such a shaman is known is 'he who knows the ways or paths of the souls'. These paths are the connections and relationships between the categorical transcendent elements or essences of which the universe is composed. The shaman's task, through his knowledge of them, is the maintenance of cosmic order (267).

In this Bororo example, we have seen the presence of two basic notions, *aroe* and *bope*, roughly translatable as essence and process, that pervade the whole universe. In human terms the former is the transcendent soul revealed in breath and names; the latter its organic existence manifest through *raka*, above all blood. Death, at the end of life, results from the final loss of all *raka* and the freeing of the soul from the decaying body. But death does not just happen; it is caused by natural processes, the *bope,* who, if it were not for the food code and the efforts of the shamans, would have destroyed human existence. Human beings are the battleground on which the war for moral and cosmic order is fought.

For my final example I want to turn to the Cashinahua who live in the Western Amazon, partly in Brazil, partly in Peru. I depend here on the 1996 article of Cecilia McCallum, entitled 'The body that knows'. In this case in order to concentrate on another aspect of the Amerindian conceptualization of the soul, I shall leave shamanism to one side, although the Cashinahua are no less immersed in shamanic ideas and practices than any other Amazonian people.

The Cashinahua think of the body as produced by others, not as growing naturally. In particular 'Growth can be defined as the corporeal accumulation of knowledge in the form of "soul".' It is this idea that I wish to examine in some detail as it seems to come so close in some ways to certain modern ideas about the development of 'consciousness'.

McCallum points out that there are two recognizable streams in the approach to the individual taken by anthropologists of Lowland South America. In one there is a tendency to oppose the biological individual to social self, and see the former as the material base on which to build a symbolic superstructure. This stream is paralleled in studies of illness and healing in which the body is understood in terms of a physical/spiritual dichotomy with herbal cures being appropriate for the first and shamanic healing for the second. In the approach she adopts the body is seen rather as the locus of the construction of sociality. Furthermore she insists there must be no separation of the physical and spiritual if we are to achieve a proper understanding of the person.

The Cashinahua body and person are created by factors external to it. This is true from the very start; the semen of the man helps build up the foetus (a very widespread idea in Lowland South America), plant medicines help the woman conceive, and she 'cooks', in Cashinahua terms, the baby in her womb. Other medicines are available to determine the sex and other qualities of the child, and to ensure easy delivery. There are the usual dietary restrictions imposed on the parents and different animals are thought to affect the child in different ways. These processes continue after the baby is born, although the application is then direct rather than mediated through the bodies of the parents. Plant medicines are applied directly in order either to promote or to prevent certain attributes. This is part of the wider process for which the Cashinahua use the Portuguese term, *experiência* [in Portuguese this word means both experience and experiment], that has the implication of both material and mental growth. The Cashinahua do not have the idea of a set field of knowledge external to the body. Rather knowledge is individual and results from a process of learning through experience. As such it is inseparable from the individual. Different bodies accumulate different knowledge as a result of their unique histories or experiences. Furthermore different parts of the body are the sites of different sorts of knowledge. Skin, hands, ears, eyes, etc., are associated with the acquisition of particular forms of knowledge and of putting that knowledge to use. There is obviously here some association with what we would call the 'senses'.

The Cashinahua do not have the concept 'mind' that can be opposed to 'body'. The powers of thinking and knowing are not situated in any specific organ – indeed the brain is not endowed with any sort of knowledge as contrasted with hands, eyes, skin, etc. Thinking and knowing are rather closely linked to the soul, which a child has from the moment of conception and which gradually grows. But it is more complex than that. The Cashinahua believe that each person has a number of souls. The true soul or eye soul is the animating principle or life, is present in the foetus, and has an other-worldly origin. They also recognize the existence of a dream soul which is not unlike the true soul and which travels during dreams. Then there is the body soul which can be equated with consciousness, memory, thought, feeling and individuality, and is in part materially derived. The body soul is fixed to the body during life, but at death turns into a monstrous faceless and memoryless forest spirit; it is mortal. The true soul may leave the body during life and at death becomes immortal in the land of the dead. Illness is a state where the true soul is loosening itself from the body but differs from death in that it is suffered in a state of consciousness. Dying is a painless and unconscious condition when the true soul leaves; once again the word for death and unconsciousness are the same.

The body soul is knowledge within the body, derived from experiences of the body parts. But the experiences of the true soul and dream soul are also part of the learning process; an agent in the accumulation of the knowledge that is the body soul. The true soul and dream soul are a sort of person within a person, and in their capacity to separate from the body they go and have experiences outside those accessible in the visible and material world and thus to the body soul. The memories of these experiences are transferred to the body soul and form part of its accumulated knowledge. Thus, proper and full knowledge requires access to both the visible and invisible aspects of the world.

To summarize this, I can do no better than to quote McCallum:

If the capacities to think and know come into being at the moment of conception . . . I interpret this to mean simply that the true soul is present in the new fetus. Consciousness and memory, however, only take substance slowly, together with the body and as a quality of the body soul. I have argued here that thinking and knowing as corporeal activities are possible when the working relationship between true and dream souls, on the one hand, and the body soul on the other, has been established. Knowing and thinking may be characterized as 'functions' of these souls' relationship only when the souls are securely integrated into a healthy, active and *conscious* body. The body is 'mind' in this compound sense, as the container of the working relationship between knowing organs and body soul, and between body soul and true soul (362).

Thus the Cashinahua can be said to recognize the presence in the person, in the form of different concepts, two of the meanings the term soul has for us; soul as mind and soul as an immortal entity. The Cashinahua do not endow the brain itself with any degree of consciousness or knowledge, but rather distribute these qualities among other parts of the body. The 'body soul', for which 'mind' might be one translation, is derived from experience whether of this or of the other world. The body soul increases with experience and together with the immortal soul constitutes the unique 'self'.

The Cashinahua example has particular value in terms of the subject matter of this volume. A happy coincidence, shortly after reading a draft of McCallum's article, was hearing a lecture by Colin Blakemore entitled 'How the environment builds the brain'. In his lecture he mentioned the idea that the brain's capability is developed by interaction with its environment. I recognized in what he said very distant but intriguing echoes of the Cashinahua material. I then discovered that Blakemore had collaborated in a work with Susan Greenfield, a contributor to this volume. This led me to her book *Journey to the Centers of the Mind,* and the discovery of some fascinating parallels between modern scientific thought and the Cashinahua ideas. Let me quote from Greenfield:

> One of the most basic features of consciousness . . . is that consciousness grows as the brain does. Consciousness is not all-or-none but increases and deepens as the brain becomes more sophisticated and as one progresses from fetus to neonate to child. In addition, it is possible to imagine that even as adults our consciousness will also be variable in depth, momentarily shrinking and expanding in accordance with our interaction with the outside world as we live out our lives (1995: x).

And:

> Everything we see, hear, taste, touch and smell is laced with associations from previous experiences. . . . As we get older, the associations are richer while some objects might trigger more associations than others. . . . Our consciousness is not an all-or-none but a variable phenomenon that grows as we do (1995: 10–11).

If in that quotation we replace brain with those parts of the Cashinuaha body that have knowledge derived from experience;

skin, hands, ears, eyes, etc., we have a statement that, one suspects, might be readily comprehensible to a Cashinahua. I hasten to add that I am not saying that the Cashinahua have developed an ur-science of consciousness, that has somehow pre-empted the findings of modern neuroscience. That is clearly not the case. What they have and, what is interesting, is a series of ideas whereby the self, the mortal self as contained in the notion of body soul, is seen as developing by the accretion of knowledge through individual experience of the world. In other words although the methods, techniques, and idioms employed by the neuroscientist and the Cashinahua are worlds apart, both have developed the notion of self based on a mind created through interaction with its environment. In both cases a dynamic idea that explains not only the self but the idiosyncracies of each self. What is also of interest is that the Cashinahua as much as the neurologist, see consciousness as a process. In the latter case nothing but process as the salvational aspect of the soul has been excluded. The Cashinahua, however, still hang on to the idea of an essence, an immortal soul, but it becomes operative, so to speak, only through interaction with the world.

There is no conclusion to be drawn from this brief survey of the ideas certain native peoples of Lowland South America have of concepts that fall roughly within the semantic range of our term 'soul'. I have rather artificially restricted myself to the human soul, and it should be remembered that in many of these societies similar qualities may be shared by all animate beings, making allowance in each case for who or what may be regarded as animate. The importance of these concepts lies not simply in the construction of the person but also in his or her relationship to past and future as well as present, and to the wider world, including the categorical order of the universe. I mentioned near the beginning of this chapter that not infrequently contact has had the effect of increasing shamanic activity. This may not now sound too surprising given the devastation that contact so often brings not simply to individual human life but to the very categorical principles, in other words the souls and essences, from which the world and everything in it are constituted. It is just these for which the shaman is responsible.

References

Chaumeil, J.-P. (1983) *Voir, savoir, pouvoir. Le chamanisme chez les Yagua du Nord-Est péruvien,* Paris: Éd. de l'École des hautes études en sciences sociales.

Crocker, J. C. (1985) *Vital Souls. Bororo Cosmology, Natural Symbolism, and Shamanism*, Tucson: University of Arizona Press.

Descola, P. (1992) 'Societies of nature and the nature of society', in A. Kuper, (ed), *Conceptualizing Society* London and New York: Routledge.

Eliade, M. (1964) *Shamanism: Archaic Techniques of Ecstasy*, New York: Bollingen Foundation.

Greenfield, S. A. (1995) *Journey to the Centers of the Mind. Toward a Science of Consciousness*, New York: W.H. Freeman and Company.

Guss, D. M. (1989). *To Weave and Sing: Art, Symbol, and Narrative in the South American Rain Forest*, Berkeley, Los Angeles, and London: University of California Press.

Harner, M. J. (1972) *The Jívaro People of the Sacred Waterfalls*. Berkeley: University of California Press.

Hugh-Jones, C. (1979) *From the Milk River. Spatial and Temporal Processes in Northwest Amazonia*, Cambridge: Cambridge University Press.

McCallum, C. (1996) 'The body that knows: from Cashinahua epistemology to a medical anthropology of Lowland South America', *Medical Anthropology Quarterly*, 10(ns): 347–72.

Overing, J. (1988) 'Personal autonomy and the domestication of the self in Piaroa society', in I. Lewis and G. Jahoda, (eds.) *Acquiring Culture*, London: Croom Helm.

Rivière, P. (1995) 'AAE na Amazônia', *Revista de Antropologia*, 38: 191–203.

Sullivan, L. E. (1988) *Icanchu's Drum. An Orientation to Meaning in South American Religions*, New York: Macmillan Publishing.

6

AUGUSTINE AND DESCARTES ON THE SOULS OF ANIMALS

Gary Matthews

In Book I, Chapter 4, of Augustine's *De musica* we find the following speculation on why birds sing:

Master: Tell me, I pray you, do not all these people seem to you to be like the nightingale who, guided by a sort of feeling, sings well, that is to say, rhythmically and sweetly, although if asked about these rhythms, or about the intervals of high and low voices, they would be unable to reply?

Disciple: I think they are very like it.

Master: What shall we say of those who take pleasure in listening to them, but are without the science [of music]? When we see elephants, bears, and certain other kinds of animals moved to sing, when we see the birds themselves delighted with their own voices – for with no other fitting purpose they would not sing so eagerly without enjoying it – are not these people [who lack the science of music] comparable to animals?[1]

(De musica 1.4.5)

Ornithologists today can be expected to offer evolutionary explanations of birdsongs. Thus, perhaps, male song sparrows tend to sing vigorously and virtuosically because vivid and virtuosic songsters among their kind are more likely to attract mates and reproduce; thus perhaps an initially quite accidental music-making mutation in a sparrow's genetic makeup will prove to have survival value. Still, the care with which song sparrows put together their songs might suggest, even to a modern ornithologist, that these birds actually take pleasure in their song. In any case, Augustine, in this passage, has no difficulty with the idea that birds take pleasure in singing, or even with the idea that they act *so as* to give themselves pleasure.

As naturally as Augustine attributes feelings of pleasure to songbirds, he just as naturally remains agnostic about the actual quality of animal experience, especially when the animal's behaviour does not fit with what his own experience would have led him to expect. Thus in Book III of the *Contra academicos* Augustine emphasizes the subjective character of taste by pointing out that the very leaves of wild olive trees that he himself finds quite unpalatable are loved by goats. 'I do not know how [those olive leaves] seem to the goat' he remarks, 'but they are bitter to me.' (*Contra academicos* 3.11.26).

Acting so as to give themselves pleasure is not the only, or even the most impressive, accomplishment Augustine attributes to nonhuman animals. Consider this passage from Book VIII of his *De trinitate*, where he offers an account of how we attribute minds, or rational souls, to others:

> For we also recognize, from a likeness to us, the motions of bodies by which we perceive that others besides us live. Just as we move [our] bodies in living, so, we notice, those bodies are moved. For when a living body is moved there is no way open to our eyes to see the mind [*animus*], a thing which cannot be seen by the eyes. But we perceive something present in that mass [*illi moli*] such as is present in us to move our mass in a similar way; it is life and soul [*anima*]. Nor is such perception something peculiar to, as it were, human prudence and reason [*quasi humanae prudentiae rationisque*]. For indeed beasts [*bestiae*] perceive as living, not only themselves, but also each other, and one another, and us as well. Nor do they see our souls [*animas*], except from the motions of the body, and they do that immediately and very simply by a sort of natural agreement [*quadam conspiratione naturali*]. Therefore we know the mind of anyone at all from our own; and from our own case we believe in that which we do not know [*ex nostro credimus quem non novimus*]. For not only do we perceive a mind [*animum*], but we even know what one is, by considering our own, for we have a mind.

> (*De trinitate* 8.6.9)

The process by which, according to Augustine, we come to perceive that other human beings have minds ('we perceive something present in that mass such as is present in us to move our mass in a similar way') is an application of an argument which has been notorious in our own day under the name 'Argument from Analogy for Other minds'. This may, in fact, be the very formulation of that argument. If it is, one would like to know why Augustine, but perhaps no one before Augustine, felt the need for an argument of this sort.

It is worth remarking at this point that Augustine in this passage is at least as much interested in the question of how we get the idea of what a mind is, as he is with establishing that there exist other minds. That makes his reasoning directly relevant to twentieth-century discussion, associated perhaps especially with Wittgenstein, of whether one could learn from one's own case what a mind is, what a pain is, and so on for other psychological or mental acts and particulars.

Augustine's answer to the question, 'How does one come to know what a mind is?' is contained in the following passage, which immediately precedes the argument from analogy for other minds I just quoted:

> And as regards the soul, we not unfittingly say that we, therefore, know what a soul is because we also have a soul. We have never seen it with our eyes, nor formed a generic or specific idea of it from any similarity with other souls that we have seen, but rather, as I said, because we also have a soul. For what is so intimately known, and what knows itself to be itself, than that through which all other things are likewise known, that is, the soul itself?
>
> (*De trinitate* 8.6.9, trans. McKenna)

Let me make a terminological comment here. Augustine uses the feminine word for soul, '*anima*', more broadly than the masculine form, '*animus*'. In fact, he uses the masculine form, which we could translate 'rational soul', interchangeably with '*mens*' ('mind'). So we can formulate Augustine's thesis this way:

> Thesis (T): The mind of each of us knows what a mind is simply and solely by knowing itself.

An historian should be reluctant to try to identify *anything* in *any* thinker as totally original, lest someone come along and find an anticipation of that very thought in some earlier thinker. Nevertheless, I want to say that, so far as I know, Thesis (T) is original with Augustine. His commitment to Thesis (T) sets up the problem of other minds for him. Therefore the fact that Thesis (T) is, apparently, first found in Augustine helps explain why the argument from analogy for other minds is also, apparently, first stated in him. Let me pause here, briefly, to expand on this last point. If I know what a mind is, and what pains, tastes, feelings, and other mental particulars are, simply and solely from an intimate and direct knowledge of my own mind and the pains, tastes, feelings, and so on, that I myself have, the question naturally arises, 'On what basis can I attribute minds and mental particulars to other beings?' The answer the argument from analogy provides is this: 'I note correlations between, on the one hand, the contents of my own mind and, on the other, certain movements of my body, expressions on my face, and so forth; when I note similar movements of other bodies and similar expressions on other faces, I infer, by analogy, that there are minds to go with those other bodies and there are similar mental particulars that make up the contents of those other minds.'

Questions surrounding Thesis (T) call for much, much more discussion than this; but I cannot provide that discussion here. My subject is animal souls. So I must focus our attention again on what Augustine says about animals in his presentation of the argument from analogy for other minds.

What exactly Augustine supposes that non-human animals do when they 'see our souls . . . immediately and very simply by a sort of natural agreement [*conspiratione naturali*]' is not immediately clear. Perhaps his insistence on the claim that they do what they do 'immediately and very simply by a sort of natural agreement' rules out the idea of a formal inference. But we do not even know whether Augustine supposes that *all* human beings formulate for themselves a formal inference to the conclusion that there are other minds. Perhaps he thinks only philosophers do that. So far as we know, Augustine may suppose that some human beings, or perhaps even all human beings *some of the time* directly perceive analogies between their movements and those of other beings just the way beasts do, that is, 'immediately and very simply by a sort of natural agreement'.

In any case, Augustine clearly thinks beasts can do something that at least *resembles* what a human being might do as a result of making an analogical inference. Augustine's claim reminds me of interesting research by David Premack and Guy Woodruff some years ago summarized in a fascinating article of theirs, 'Does the chimpanzee have a theory of mind?'[2] What the Premack–Woodruff experiments seem to reveal is chimpanzees putting themselves vicariously in the place of human beings and solving simple, practical problems for those human beings.

The use Augustine makes of the argument from analogy for other minds is important for understanding Augustine's view of non-human animals in two different ways. First, as I have just been emphasizing, Augustine attributes to non-human animals themselves the ability to deploy the argument from analogy, or at least to do something very much like actually deploying that argument. Second, by deploying the argument to justify a belief in the existence of souls other than his own, he leaves himself open to seeing similarities, not just between his own behaviour and that of other human beings, but also between human and animal souls On this last point Augustine would have to agree with David Hume, who writes: "Tis from the resemblance of the external actions of animals to those we ourselves perform, that we judge their internal likewise to resemble ours.'[3]

All this might seem unremarkable and rather humdrum if it were not for the fact that Descartes, whose views about the human mind seem in many respects quite Augustinian, claims that non-human animals are only soul-less machines. When I say that Descartes's views about the human mind seem to be very Augustinian, I have in mind Augustinian ideas such as are expressed in the following passage from Book X of Augustine's *De trinitate*, a passage in which Augustine is trying to refute those philosophers who suppose the mind is something material:

> All of these people overlook the fact that the mind [*mens*] knows itself, even when it seeks itself, as we have already shown. But we can in no way rightly say that anything is known while its essence [*substantia*] is unknown. Wherefore, as long as the mind knows itself, it knows its own essence [*substantia*]. But it is certain about itself, as what we have already said clearly demonstrates. But it is by no means certain whether it is air, or fire, or a body, or anything of a body. It is, therefore, none of these things.
>
> (*De trinitate* 10.10.16)

I should say that I have substituted 'essence' for 'substance' in Stephen McKenna's otherwise fine translation of this passage[4] on the grounds that (1) Augustine makes clear elsewhere in the same work that he understands the philosophical meaning of the Latin word '*substantia*' to be indifferent as between 'essence' and 'substance' and (2) 'essence' seems to be what is crucial here. On the first point, Augustine writes in Book V of the *De trinitate* that 'the usage of our language has already decided that the same thing is to be understood when we say *essentia* as when we say *substantia*' (*De trinitate* 5.9.10). As for the second point, Augustine's idea seems to be that the mind couldn't just *happen* to be something corporeal. If it is something corporeal, the reasoning seems to go, it is something *essentially* corporeal.

A reader familiar with Descartes may be put in mind by all this of such passages as the following one from *Meditation* II:

> What else am I? I will use my imagination. I am not that structure of limbs which is called a human body. I am not even some thin vapour which permeates the limbs – a wind, fire, air, breath, or whatever I depict in my imagination; for these are things which I have supposed to be nothing. Without changing this supposition, I find that I am still certain that I am something.[5]

Descartes, as we know, concludes that he is a mind, a thinking thing (*res cogitans*), that is, 'a thing that doubts, understands, affirms, denies, is willing, is unwilling, and also imagines and has sensory perceptions.'[6] In a similar spirit, Augustine concludes that he is something that 'lives,[7] remembers, understands, wills, thinks, knows, and judges' (*De trinitate* 10.10.14).

Given this similarity between Augustine's and Descartes's views of themselves as minds, or rational souls, the discrepancy between their treatment of animal souls is simply staggering. In fact, the extent of Descartes's break with his predecessors, apparently *all* his predecessors, on the question of animal souls can hardly be exaggerated. My favourite way of bringing this out appeals to what I call the idea of 'the unity of psychology.' By 'the unity of psychology' I mean something one might also express by saying that the psychology of human beings is part of the psychology of animals generally.

There are several different ways of trying to trace out the ramifications of the idea that psychology is one. A central consideration, I think, is likely to be some sort of principle of continuity up and down the scale of nature. The idea would be that up and down the scale of animated or ensouled things (Greek: *empsycha*, 'enpsyched' things) there are always psychological continuities, never any strict discontinuity. If human beings can get angry, see an illusion, entertain a belief, or develop an Oedipus complex, then so can some lower animal do either the very same thing, something similar, or at least something analogous.

It is perhaps useful to speak of a psychological act, state, or function in a lower animal as *being a model of*, or as *modeling*, a state, act, or function in a higher animal when the former is either the very same kind of thing as the latter, a similar kind of thing to the latter, or at least something analogous to the latter. The Principle of Psychological Continuity is then the principle that psychological acts, states, and functions in lower animals *model* those in higher animals.[8]

Plato and Aristotle, I should say, both accepted the Principle of Psychological Continuity, but the basis upon which Aristotle accepted this principle was very different from that on which Plato accepted it. Plato took over the Pythagorean idea of metempsychosis. It is possible, he thought, that your psyche or mine might next animate a dog, or a fish, or even a bee. On this view, psychological acts, states, and functions in lower animals are like those in higher animals for the very good reason that the psyches of lower animals are, or may be, degenerate human psyches. In fact, Plato sometimes suggests that the soul of a given person may, in its next incarnation, go into some animal whose characteristic virtues and vices are most like those the person had developed in the present life.[9]

Aristotle accepted the Principle of Psychological Continuity on quite a different basis. His threefold classification of psyches – (1) plant or nutritive souls, (2) animal or sensitive souls, and (3) human or rational souls – already incorporates limited continuity, since Aristotle supposed that the psychic functions of human souls include both sensitive and nutritive functions, and the functions of animal souls include nutritive functions.[10] But the Aristotelian classification scheme also suggests radical discontinuity. It suggests that there is nothing in plants similar or analogous to sensation in animals, and, more to our purpose, nothing in non-human animals similar or analogous to reason in human beings.

Aristotle counters the suggestion of discontinuity in his classification scheme in various places, but nowhere more eloquently than in this famous passage from the beginning of Book VIII of the *History of Animals*:

> In the great majority of animals there are traces of psychical qualities or attitudes, which qualities are more markedly

differentiated in the case of human beings. For just as we pointed out resemblances in the physical organs, so so in a number of animals we observe gentleness or fierceness, mildness or cross temper, courage or timidity, fear or confidence, high spirit or low cunning, and, with regard to intelligence, something equivalent to sagacity. Some of these qualities in human beings, as compared with the corresponding qualities in animals, differ only quantitatively; that is to say, a human being has more or less of this quality, and an animal has more or less of some other; other qualities in human beings are represented by analogous and not identical qualities; for instance, just as in human beings we find knowledge, wisdom, and sagacity, so in certain animals there exists some other natural potentiality akin to these ... so that one is quite justified in saying that, as regards human beings and animals, certain psychical qualities are identical with one another, whilst others resemble, and others are analogous to each other.

(588a18–b3, trans. Barnes)

One can hardly imagine a better elaboration on the Principle of Psychological Continuity, or a better statement of the general idea of the Unity of Psychology. As for Augustine, he never makes any pronouncement as general as this on psychological continuity; still, the remarks on non-human animals that he scatters throughout his writings suggest that, in this respect anyway, he would have little to disagree with Aristotle about.

It is against the background of Aristotelian and Platonic assumptions about psychological continuity that Descartes insists on a radical discontinuity between the human mind and the animator of non-human creatures. In the reply to Gassendi, *Reply to Objections* V, Descartes is blunt:

The next question you raise concerns the obscurity arising from the ambiguity in the word 'soul' ... primitive man probably did not distinguish between, on the one hand, the principle by which we are nourished and grow and accomplish without any thought all the other operations which we have in common with the brutes, and, on the other hand, the principle in virtue of which we think. He therefore used the single term 'soul' to apply to both; and when he subsequently noticed that thought was distinct from nutrition, he

called the element which thinks 'mind', and believed it to be
the principle part of the soul. I, by contrast, realizing that
the principle by which we are nourished is wholly different
– different in kind – from that in virtue of which we think,
have said that the term 'soul', when it is used to refer to both
these principles, is ambiguous. If we are to take 'soul' in its
special sense, as meaning the 'first actuality' or 'principle
form of man', then the term must be understood to apply
only to the principle in virtue of which we think; and to
avoid ambiguity I have as for as possible used the term
'mind' for this. For I consider the mind not as a part of the
soul but as the thinking soul in its entirety.[11]

By denying that non-human animals have psyches in the same
sense in which human beings have them, and by, therefore, denying
that non-human beings have psychological acts, states and functions
in the same sense in which human beings have them, Descartes
rejects the Principle of Psychological Continuity. To be sure, he
accepts a principle of *behavioural* continuity. In fact, supposing, as
he does, that living animals are machines of a sort, he supposes not
only that their behaviour models human behavior, but also that the
behaviour of mechanical artifacts models the behaviour of living
animals, as he declares in, for example, these passages:

Doubtless when the swallows come in Spring, they operate
like clocks. The actions of honey bees are of the same nature,
and the discipline of cranes in flight, and of apes in fighting,
if it is true that they keep discipline.
(Letter to the Marquess of Newcastle, 1646)[12]

[Y]ou seem to make a greater difference between living and
lifeless things than there is between a clock or other
automaton on the one hand, and a key or sword or other
non-self-moving appliance on the other. I do not agree.
(Letter to Regius, 1643)[13]

Some people have tried to soften the force of Descartes's distinction between things that are capable of consciousness and those that
are not. The modern notion of consciousness and the concept of
mind that goes with it are, to a great extent, inventions of Descartes.
They have their natural home in the context of his Rational
Reconstruction of Knowledge and in his use of the Method of

Systematic Doubt. Thus the mind is, for Descartes, something he can be certain he is and can be certain exists even when, in the throes of Systematic Doubt, he brings himself to doubt that bodies even exist. When Descartes denies mind and consciousness to non-human animals he is using technical terminology, so this reasoning goes, to mark dramatically a distinction that we might otherwise have overlooked or underemphasized.

Such an effort to soften the force of Descartes's distinction between the minded and the mindless is, in my opinion, misguided. One thing that shows it to be misguided is Descartes's own insistence that the first principle of action in a living, but mindless, being is a mechanical principle quite like the mechanical principle of a watch or other automaton.

What kind of attitude is appropriate to the consideration of a fine watch? One might be appropriately ravished into admiration for the watchmaker. One might be pleased by the watch's design or annoyed by its undependability. But one family of attitudes would clearly be inappropriate, no matter how finely wrought the watch, or how dependable its action – namely, those attitudes of sympathy and concern which one may have for the feelings of another conscious being.

When Descartes insists that the first principle of action in a living, but non-human, being is a mechanical principle quite like that of a wound-up watch, we must conclude that, according to him, attitudes of sympathy and concern for the feelings of x are clearly inappropriate where x is only a goldfish, or even a dog or chimpanzee; their souls are mechanical. It is this last point that should keep us from dismissing as simply scurrilous the stories of cruelty to animals told of the Cartesians at Port Royal. 'They administered beatings to dogs with perfect indifference,' we are told,

> and made fun of those who pitied the creatures as if they felt pain. They said the animals were clocks; that the cries they emitted when struck were only the noise of a little spring that had been touched, but that the whole body was without feeling. They nailed the poor animals up on boards by their four paws to vivisect them and see the circulation of the blood which was a great subject of controversy.[14]

Why did Descartes make the claim of radical discontinuity between the psychology of human beings and the 'psychology' of non-human animals? Various suggestions have been offered. I have made one of my own.[15] Perhaps the most interesting candidate, however, is exemplified by Donald Davidson's reasoning in his paper, 'Rational Animals.'[16] Davidson recalls Norman Malcolm's story of the dog chasing a cat up a tree. When the dog continues to bark excitedly, we may say, 'He thinks that the cat went up the tree.' But Davidson demurs.

For our comment to be correct, Davidson thinks,

> the dog must believe, under some description of the tree, that the cat went up that tree. But what kind of description would suit the dog? For example, can the dog believe of an object that it is a tree? This would seem impossible unless we suppose that the dog has many . . . beliefs about trees: that they are growing things, that they need soil and water, that they have leaves or needles, that they burn. There is no fixed list of things someone with the concept of tree must believe, but without many [such] beliefs, there would be no reason to identify a belief as a belief about a tree, much less an oak tree. Similar considerations apply to the dog's supposed thinking about the cat.[17]

Davidson's view (it has also been the view of other philosophers) is that, to have a belief about a tree – for example, the belief that the cat when up a tree – a dog would need to have a concept of a tree; moreover, to have a concept of a tree, the dog would have to have a network of beliefs about trees. But, since the dog can't be said to have a network of beliefs about trees (for example, that they are growing things, need soil and water, etc.) it can't have the thought that the cat went up the tree.

A related way of expressing this sort of worry is to be found in an earlier article by Stephen Stich. Beliefs have content, Stich points out. The belief that the cat went up the tree includes in its content the concept of a cat and the concept of a tree. The concept of a tree is fixed by certain minimal botanical information and the concept of cat by certain minimal zoological information. Since the dog lacks both sorts of information, the dog cannot have the belief that the cat went up the tree, or have any such thought.

What beings have enough information to fix concepts to make it possible for them to think, and to have beliefs? It is plausible to suppose that the only creatures that can do that are creatures that speak a real language. This line of reasoning is, I think, the one that makes most plausible Descartes's claim that 'speech is the only certain sign of thought hidden in a body.'[18]

On this reasoning, then, Descartes was right to draw a clear line between those creatures capable of holding the belief that *p*, and those that, apparently, can do no such thing. And he was right in thinking that it is the language-users and only the language-users that clearly can entertain thoughts and hold beliefs; the non-language-users, apparently, are incapable of thinking that *p*. A further implication of this line of reasoning is that, since it is only language-users whose behaviour is mediated by thinking, the Principle of the Unity of Psychology is false.

Let us return, now, to Augustine. Although Augustine anticipated Descartes in formulating the *cogito* and in supposing that the mind is a thinking thing, he did not, like Descartes, suppose that non-human animals are soul-less brutes. 'If those animals were soul-less beings [*exanimes*],' he has Evodius say in the early treatise, *On Free Choice of the Will* (*De libero arbitrio*), 'then I might say we are superior to them because we have a soul' (1.7). To Evodius, and to Augustine as well, it is obvious that any animal, whether human or not, is animated by an *anima*, a soul. And there is for him no equivocation in saying that a dog and a human being each have an *anima*.

Moreover, as we have already seen, Augustine attributes rather sophisticated intellectual capacities to beasts, including the capacity to attribute, by a perceived analogy, souls or minds to other beasts, as well as to us human beings. What he denies that they have is much self-knowledge, even the knowledge that they live, or that they exist.[19] And he denies that they reason.

So beasts are, for Augustine as well as for Descartes, non-rational animals. But in what respect does Augustine think that non-human animals fall short of rationality? Perhaps his most interesting suggestion as to what the non-rationality of beasts consists in is that they lack free choice. That seems to be the main content of the following passage from Augustine's long commentary on the book of *Genesis*, *De genesi ad litteram*:

> All living souls, not only rational souls as in human beings, but also irrational souls as in cattle, birds, and fishes, are moved by what they see. But a rational soul by a free choice of the will either assents to what it sees or fails to assent. An irrational soul, however, does not have this power of judgment, but affected by something seen, it is set in motion according to its kind and nature.
>
> (9.14.25)

One implication of this is that the basic distinction between human beings and non-human animals is, in effect, a moral one. We human beings may have moral obligations to beasts to, for example, reduce their suffering. But they have no reciprocal moral obligations to us, or to each other. Being systematically unable to do anything other than gratify their desires, they fall short of moral agency. Richard Sorabji, in his treatment of Augustine on animals in his Townsend Lectures, *Animal Minds and Human Morals*,[20] emphasizes a passage from *The City of God* in which Augustine justifies killing animals on the ground that they have no rational community with us human beings. In this passage Augustine explains that the Divine prohibition against killing ('Thou shalt not kill!') is not about

> irrational living things, whether flying, swimming, walking, or crawling, because they are not associated in a community (*sociantur*) with us by reason (*ratio*), since it is not given to them to have reason in common (*communis*) with us. Hence it is by a very just ordinance of the Creator that their life and death is subordinated to ours.
>
> (*De civitate dei* 1.20)[21]

The community of reason Augustine has in mind here is not a society of philosophers, but rather a society of moral agents able to exercise free will in the service of practical reason.

If Augustine denies moral agency to animals, as he clearly does, does he thereby also reject the Principle of Psychological Continuity? I think not. It is open to him to maintain that non-human animals, though incapable of free choice of the will and thus incapable of real moral virtue, are nevertheless quite capable of doing things in a way that mimics morally virtuous, as well as morally vicious, behaviour. Such a position seems to fit well with the homiletical and exegetical use Augustine makes of animal examples, as in this passage from *On Diverse Questions* 83:

> Just as some people, zealous of acquiring such knowledge, recount of stags, that when a herd crosses over a body of water to an island for the purpose of feeding, the stags so arrange themselves that they support by turn the burden of their heads, which are heavy with the weight of their horns; and they do this in such a manner that each stag places his outstretched head on the back of the stag in front of him. And since of necessity the one preceding all the

others has no support before him on which to rest his head, they are said to assume this position by turns; so that the one which preceded the others, when wearied by the weight of his head, retires behind all the others, and his place is taken by one whose head he was supporting when he was in the first place himself. Thus bearing one another's burdens by turn, they cross over the water to solid land. Solomon perhaps had this custom of the stags in mind when he said, 'Let the stag of friendship . . . have converse with you,' for nothing so [much] proves friendship as the bearing of a friend's burden.

(71.1, trans. Mosher)

My suggestion is then that, whereas Descartes's views are clearly incompatible with the Principle of Psychological Continuity, Augustine's are not. To be sure, both philosophers claim rationality as what marks off human from non-human animals. But, whereas Descartes considers non-rational animals to be mere machines, Augustine thinks of their sentience and even their quasi-intellectual capacities as quite analogous to ours. He even supposes they are capable of behavior that models human altruism.

In a letter of 23 November 1646 to the Marquess of Newcastle Descartes writes:

the reason why animals do not speak as we do is not that they lack the organs but that they have no thoughts. It cannot be said that they speak to each other and that we cannot understand them; because since dogs and some other animals express their passions to us, they would express their thoughts also if they had any.[22]

Augustine, by contrast, is prepared to see an analogy between sign use in non-human animals and language in human beings, as in this passage from his On Christian Doctrine:

Even beasts have certain signs among themselves by which they make known the desires of their mind. For the barn-yard cock, having found a bit of food, gives a signal with his voice to the hen that she may come running; the dove calls its mate by cooing, or in turn is called by her; and many signs of this sort are commonly observed.

(2.3, trans. Pine-Coffin)

Let's return to the Davidson/Stich-type reasoning, according to which we have no basis for attributing thought to a speechless animal, since there is no reason to suppose that, for example, the dog thinks that the cat went up the tree *rather than* that the 'fuzzy thing' went up the log, or the animal that keeps saying 'meow' went up the pole, or any one of an indefinitely large number of other alternatives.

I myself think that there are usually good ways to pare down the content we attribute to, say, the thoughts of dogs when we credit them with thinking. Thus we might want to strip down the content of a dog's thought, 'The cat went up the tree,' to yield the double *de re* belief of the object, *that* (dog), and the place, *there* (in the tree), that *that* is *there*, that is, is located *there*. But I shall not try to spell out here just what store of concepts and therefore what range of belief-contents it might be reasonable to credit a moderately intelligent dog with.

Rather than haggle over whether dog behaviour is or is not sufficiently differentiated to credit dogs with this or that concept, with, for example, the concept of a chewable thing, if not with the concept of a bone, I think it would be wise to criticize the Davidson/Stich position more directly. The main trouble with their line of reasoning, I suggest, is that it leaves us unable to understand how human infants ever *acquire* a language.

If B. F. Skinner had been successful in giving an account of language-acquisition through operant conditioning, we wouldn't need to suppose that the infant language-learner needs to frame and test hypotheses to learn a language. But Noam Chomsky has shown, I take it, that a Skinnerian approach to understanding language acquisition is bound to fail.[23] As things stand, then, we can put forward this simple argument with considerable confidence:

Argument A
1   Anyone who can learn a language is already able to think.
2   Pre-linguistic human infants can learn a language.
Therefore,
3   Pre-linguistic human infants are already able to think.

No such argument as this is ever stated by Augustine; nevertheless, the ideas behind it are reflected in Augustine's account of his own acquisition of language – an account made famous by Wittgenstein:

[L]ater on I realized how I had learnt to speak. It was not my elders who showed me the words by some set system of instruction, in the way that they taught me to read not long

afterwards; but, instead, I taught myself by using the intelligence which you, my God, gave to me. For when I tried
to express my meaning by crying out and making various
sounds and movements, so that my wishes would be obeyed,
I found that I could not convey all that I meant or make
myself understood by everyone whom I wished to understand me. So my memory prompted me. I noticed that
people would name some object and then turn towards
whatever it was that they had named. I watched them and
understood that the sound they made when they wanted to
indicate that particular thing was the name which they gave
to it, and their actions clearly showed what they meant,
. . . So, by learning the words arranged in various phrases
and constantly repeated, I gradually pieced together what
they stood for, and when my tongue had mastered the pro-
nunciation, I began to express my wishes by means of them.

(*Confessions* 1.8)

Wittgenstein has, of course, brought out various difficulties with
the picture of language learning Augustine presents in this passage.
Some of those difficulties, and especially the problem of the ambiguity of ostension, and hence the problem of learning the meaning
of words by having examples of things they can be applied to pointed
out to us, are confronted by Augustine himself in his dialogue, *De
magistro*. But my point is not that Augustine had a philosophically
satisfactory account of language learning, only that he correctly
supposed that an infant must already be able to think for it to be
able to learn a language.

Of course, Descartes would have happily conceded that a pre-
linguistic infant can think. Supposing, as he did, that a mind is an
essentially thinking thing and that even a foetus in its mother's
womb has a mind, he had to suppose that a foetus thinks. And that
is exactly what he says, for example, in this letter to Hyperaspistes
of August, 1641:

I had reason to assert that the human soul, wherever it be,
even in the mother's womb, is always thinking. What more
certain or evident reason could be wished for than the one
I gave? I had proved that the nature or essence of soul
consists in the fact that it is thinking, just as the essence
of body consists in the fact that it is extended. Now nothing
can ever be deprived of its own essence; so it seems to me

that a man who denies that his soul was thinking at times when he does not remember noticing it thinking, deserves no more attention than a man who denied that his body was extended while he did not notice that it had extension. This does not mean that I believe that the mind of an infant meditates on metaphysics in its mother's womb; . . . if one may conjecture on such an unexplored topic, it seems most reasonable to think that a mind newly united to an infant's body is wholly occupied in perceiving or feeling the ideas of pain, pleasure, heat, cold and other similar ideas which arise from its union and intermingling with the body. Nonetheless, it has in itself the ideas of God, itself, and all such truths as are called self-evident, in the same way as adult humans have when they are not attending to them.[24]

So when Descartes says that speech is the only sure sign of thought hidden in a body he must mean only that speech is a *sufficient* condition of thinking, but not also a *necessary* condition. Why then is Descartes so confident that, whereas all human animals, including fetuses in the womb, have minds and can think, yet no non-human animal has a mind or can think?

As we have already noted, Descartes thinks that dogs 'would express their thoughts . . . if they had any.' His reasoning must, then, be something like this:

Argument B
1   Any creature that can think will naturally come to express its thoughts in language.
2   Dogs (for example) do not naturally come to express their thoughts in language.
Therefore,
3   Dogs cannot think.

I have been careful to add 'naturally' to 'will come to express its thought in language'. As Descartes realized, there are human mutes who can think, but, for some special reason, cannot express those thoughts in speech. The idea would be that some unnatural impediment prevents them from doing what they would otherwise do quite naturally.

Argument B is not the most illuminating argument we could have wished for on this topic. Why is it the case, we want to know – if indeed it is the case – that any creature that can think will

naturally come to express its thoughts in language? Still, even if
Argument B is not as illuminating as we could have wished, it
might, for all we have said so far, be sound. Is it?

The major trouble with Argument B, I think, is its first premise.
Consider the various cases of feral, or wild, children – children abandoned or lost as infants and raised by wolves or gazelles or other
non-human animals – or kept in solitary confinement throughout
childhood and treated as mere animals.[25] In their infancy these
children could think. In fact, they continued to be able to think.
Yet, lacking a linguistic community in which to grow up, they
never came to express their thoughts in language. What their
example shows, I think, is that language acquisition is, for members
of our species, a form of acculturation, and not something that each
intelligent human being achieves in some purely natural way, even
if left alone. So Argument B fails.

What is the upshot? Each effort by Descartes and each of our
best efforts on Descartes's behalf to draw a clean line between the
thinkers and the non-thinkers in the animal world fails. As a persua-
sive way to reject the Unity of Psychology and refute the Principle
of Psychological Continuity, Cartesianism itself fails.

The defeat of Cartesianism is a victory for Augustinianism. For,
whereas Augustine's thoughts about minds and thinking are in
many respects Cartesian, they are quite unlike Descartes's in being
entirely consistent with the Principle of Psychological Continuity.
And in this respect Augustine's thoughts about minds and thinking
are, I should say, superior to Descartes's.

Notes

1 Otherwise unattributed translations of Augustine are my own.
2 *Brain and Behavioral Sciences* 1 (1978): 515–26.
3 *A Treatise on Human Nature*, Book I, Part III, § 16.
4 Saint Augustine, *The Trinity*, *The Fathers of the Church*, v. 45,
  Washington, DC: Catholic University Press, 1963, 309.
5 *The Philosophical Writings of Descartes* (Hereafter 'CSM'), trans.
  J. Cottingham, R. Stoothoff, and D. Murdoch, vol. II, 18, using the
  translation of the French version for the concluding sentence.
6 CSM II, 19.
7 The occurrence of 'lives' here calls for comment. Certainly living is
  not something Descartes includes among the functions of a thinking
  thing. But, since in the last book of this work (*De trinitate* 15.12.21)
  Augustine asserts, on the basis of *cogito*-like reasoning, that he cannot
  doubt that he *lives*, the meaning of 'life' and 'lives' seems to be here
  rather like the meaning of 'life' in the familiar question, 'Is there life
  after death?' We can ask that question without wanting to know

whether we will perform biological functions after death. We want to know whether we will *exist* after we die.

8 For a fuller treatment of these issues, see my 'Animals and the unity of psychology,' *Philosophy* 53 (1978): 437–54.
9 *Phaedo* 81d–82b.
10 *De anima* 2.3.
11 CSM II, 246.
12 Descartes, *Philosophical Letters* [hereafter 'K'], trans. and ed. Anthony Kenny, Oxford: Clarendon Press, 1970, 207.
13 K 133.
14 Leonora Rosenfield, *From Beast-Machine to Man-Machine*, New York: Columbia, 1968, 54.
15 Matthews, 'Animals and The unity of psychology', 453–54.
16 *Actions and Events*, ed. E. Lepore and B. McLaughlin, Oxford: Blackwell, 1985, 473–80.
17 Ibid. 475.
18 Letter to More, 5 February 1649, K 245.
19 *De libero arbitrio* 1.7.
20 *Animal Minds and Human Morals: The Origins of the Western Debate*, Ithaca, NY: Cornell University Press, 1993, 195–8.
21 Translation in Sorabji, ibid. 197.
22 K 207.
23 See Chomsky's review of Skinner's *Verbal Behavior* in *Language* 35 (1959): 26–58.
24 K 111.
25 See Lucien Malson, *Wolf Children and the Problem of Human Nature*, New York: Monthly Review Press, 1972.

References

Aristotle, *History of Animals*

Augustine, *Confessiones, Contra academicos, De civitate dei, De diversis quaestionibus 83, De genesi ad litteram, De libero arbitrio, De musica, De trinitate.*

Davidson, Donald, 'Rational animals', in E. Lepore and B. McLaughlin (eds), *Actions and Events*, Oxford: Blackwell, 1985.

Descartes, *Meditations and Replies to Objections, Letters*

Premack, David, and Woodruff, Guy, 'Does the chimpanzee have a theory of mind?' *Brain and Behavioral Sciences* 1 (1978): 515–26.

Malson, Lucien, *Wolf Children and the Problem of Human Nature*, New York: Monthly Review Press, 1972.

Matthews, Gareth B., 'Animals and the unity of psychology', *Philosophy* 53 (1978): 437–54.

Rosenfield, Leonora, *From Beast–Machine to Man–Machine*, New York: Columbia, 1968.

Sorabji, Richard, *Animals Minds and Human Morals: The Origins of the Western Debate*, Ithaca: Cornell University Press, 1993.

Wittgenstein, Ludwig, *Philosophical Investigations*, trans. G. E. M. Anscombe, Oxford: Blackwell, 1967.

7

SOUL, BRAIN AND MIND

Susan Greenfield

How can a scientist have anything to say worthwhile about the soul? In recent years an increasing number have started to do just that. For example, Paul Churchland, a world expert in computation in the University of California, San Diego entitled his book *The Engine of Reason, the Seat of the Soul*[1] (Churchland 1995), whilst the cover of Francis Crick's book *The Astonishing Hypothesis*[2], actually claims to offer a 'scientific' search for the soul. If a theologian were to open these books, in pursuit of the soul, they might be dismayed to discover that such scientific forays have nothing at all to say about the quintessential feature, *immortality* of the soul, but rather focus on the mind, brain and consciousness.

Scientists are concerned with the individual, a 'mortal soul', which could be more accurately equated with mind or consciousness. What I would like to address in this chapter is how far we, as scientists, can go any way towards throwing light on what might be the mortal soul. I would like to make two initial assumptions, however. One is that the brain itself generates consciousness, which is not beamed in from outside. The second assumption might upset some philosophers, as it is that there is no ready definition for consciousness. Our starting point is the human brain: but it does not immediately yield up very many secrets. Many scientists weigh in straight away with their electrodes or their microscopes, or whatever happens to be in their area of expertise. They do look at a property or mechanism in the brain that is sufficiently novel to possibly be equated in some way with the strange and novel phenomenon of consciousness. But surely what one needs to establish first is what it is we are going to ask of the brain. What properties of consciousness could there possibly be that we are going to try and accommodate in such an unhelpful organ, with no intrinsic moving parts?

The first property is prompted simply by looking at a brain. Even to non-neuroscientists it is easy to see that it is not homogeneous, but divided into discernibly gross different brain regions (see Figure 1). For example, there is a cauliflower-shaped structure at the back, incidentally called the 'cerebellum', or little brain. There is a core-like, stalk-like structure, the brain stem, and finally there is a convoluted outer area, the cortex, named after the Latin for bark, because it appears to wrap around the brain. For many years the key question about the brain has been: what is the function of such and such an area, or more importantly is some particular structure the 'centre' for memory, or the 'centre' for emotions? The issue of localization is an intriguing yet elusive one in neuroscience. The first issue, therefore, concerns the centre for consciousness. Is there a kind of mini-brain within a brain? The reasons for rejecting this idea, a seat of a 'soul' within the brain, comes from what we know about how the brain processes its different functions. Thanks to advanced imaging techniques we can actually have a window on the living brain of a conscious person and see which parts are working hardest by means of radioactive labels which tag the parts of the

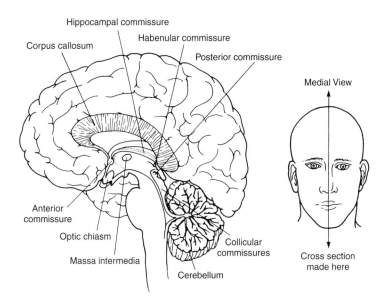

Figure 1 Scheme of the human brain

Source: Sperry, 'The great cerebral commissure' *Scientific American* (1964), in S. Springer and G. Deutsch, *Left Brain, Right Brain*

brain consuming most oxygen or glucose. In a conscious subject we can ask them to perform different aspects of a language task, namely to passively view words, speak words, listen to words, or generate verbs, in each case, different areas of the brain light up (Posner and Raichle 1994). No single brain area has a monopoly on being the language 'centre'. This type of finding is occurring all the time. People are reporting similar kinds of results with vision, movement and memory, and hence have embraced the concept of 'parallel processing', where any seeming holistic global function in the brain is actually distributed over many brain regions.

So where does parallel processing leave us with consciousness? Quite simply, we can say that no single brain region is singularly committed to generating consciousness. On the other hand, there is a problem: most people claim to experience just one type of consciousness, a cohesive state at any one moment. We have just seen that in anatomical terms consciousness is potentially multiple, and yet there is a unity to it. What I would suggest, therefore, as the first possible property of consciousness, is *it is spatially multiple*, somehow distributed all over the brain. We will worry about how parts of the brain have the potential for consciousness later: let us merely assume that, somehow, something happens in your brain that privileges one area to somehow act as the physical substitute for consciousness at any one moment.

Let us turn to a second property, prompted by considering the riddle of animal consciousness. Some people, though in a shrinking minority, might think, like Descartes, that animals are mere automata, whilst others, especially pet owners, I am sure would violently oppose the idea. On the other hand, could we say that a dog has the same type of consciousness as a human? Moreover, what about a rat? Rats are notoriously proficient at survival: they will adapt very quickly to any situation. For example, if they are offered a novel food they will wait a while, even if they are hungry, before taking too much in case it has adverse effects. They are highly proficient at immediate and specific one-off interaction with the outside world. So, although a rat has a relatively small brain, are we to think of it as a kid of furry automaton? But if we accept that a rat is conscious, is it as conscious as a chimpanzee? A chimpanzee has only a 1 per cent difference in its DNA from us. Obviously, one cannot prove that a chimpanzee is conscious but it is very hard to view its behaviour as robotic. But if one says that chimps are conscious, is it a comparable consciousness to, say, George Bernard Shaw?

This is a problem that is certainly not new: if we claim that animals are conscious, are they then as conscious as we are? What I would like to suggest is a compromise: instead of thinking of consciousness as all or none, as people tend to do, what if consciousness was a continuum, like a dimmer switch, enabling different degrees of consciousness. I would like to suggest, therefore, that a second property of consciousness is that it is variable. In primitive, or very simple brains, the level of consciousness is low, but it can grow as the brain develops. One can take this idea further, not only on the phylogenetic scale, but also in our own ontogenetic development. Again, a problem prompted by considering consciousness and the mind is the type of consciousness displayed by babies.

No scenario seems satisfactory. One possibility, that during the birth process consciousness occurs, is hard to imagine. The actual brain during birth does not undergo any very clear difference, before and after, from when it is in the womb to becoming a few minutes old as an independent entity. Alternatively, are we going to say that consciousness comes during development? I doubt very much if anyone could claim that from the first few months of life that children were not conscious at all. Neither scenario is really acceptable. However, if consciousness is continuous and variable, then one can immediately see a way forward. As the brain gets more complex in the womb, then, like a dimmer switch, consciousness gradually grows and burgeons until, of course, in adulthood it reaches its particular pinnacles or depths.

If consciousness is variable, then even as an adult, it is going to vary from one moment to the next. I would like to suggest that you do not have a fixed, immutable level of consciousness, but rather that it is variable. This idea is not particularly heretical. People are often talking about 'raising', or 'deepening', or 'blunting' their consciousness. We are quite comfortable in our folk-lore vocabulary of talking of these kind of terms: I am merely formalizing an intuitively comfortable concept.

What about a third property ? Consider 'The Fool' in the Tarot cards. He is always shown oblivious to the dog barking at his heels, and oblivious to the fact that he is about to throw himself off a cliff, because his consciousness is centred on a butterfly. This image captures the vital issue – that when you are conscious, you are not always conscious of *everything*, but rather conscious of something: to be conscious of nothing is a paradox in terms. I would like to suggest that our third property of consciousness is that it is always derived from some kind of specific stimulus. An attractive metaphor would be of some stone being thrown into a puddle and generating ripples: something is the epicentre for your consciousness.

If one accepts these three properties of consciousness, it is possible to weave them into a definition, albeit a rather cumbersome operational one. We can then work with the descriptive framework to try and impose on the physical brain. I would like to suggest that consciousness is *spatially multiple, yet effectively single at any one time. It is an emergent property of non-specialised groups of neurons (brain cells) that are continuously variable with respect to an epicentre*, where an emergent property is taken to be a property of a collection of components that could not be attributable to any single member of those components. So, for example, a symphony is an emergent property of an orchestra, but could not be attributed directly to a trombone. A curry flavour is the emergent property of a complex dish of spices, not attributable directly to turmeric or coriander, or whatever goes into curries. So I would like to suggest that, if consciousness is variable, at any one time in the brain, under conditions that we will explore, then a group of neurons are recruited in some way around some kind of stimulus epicentre. Let us look at the concept first. Imagine that in the brain, from moment to moment, that there are groups of neurons transiently forming and reforming around some kind of epicentre, a little like blobs of mercury, or like clouds, never ever the same twice – hence one never has the same consciousness twice. Somehow the very conditions that will govern the recruitment and degree to which groups of cells are forming, will vary and hence determine the extent of the formation, and the corresponding depth of consciousness. This is the model I would like to discuss, and see whether and how it might accommodated in the brain.

First let us consider the epicentre. On its own this trigger, as we can see from the earlier definition, is not going to generate consciousness. Imagine a candyfloss machine with a stick in the centre that then gathers more and more candyfloss as time goes on. Think of the epicentre as the stick in the centre, the burgeoning candyfloss being analogous to the recruitment of the cells. The stick in itself is not the candyfloss, it is just the trigger for it, just as the stone does not *contain* ripples but causes their generation. What in the brain could mediate this epicentre, this trigger? Another rather simplistic analogy might be a boss, at the centre of a big organisation that is eventually going to recruit managers and submanagers. What in the brain could be the equivalent of the boss? The most obvious candidate, and one that might immediately spring to mind, is the basic component of the brain, the neuron, or brain cell. The adult human has a hundred billion neurons, with on average between ten and one hundred thousand connections from one neuron to the next. Therefore, for simple economic reasons, it might seen appropriate for one neuron to serve as one epicentre. In the old days neuroscientists thought that one could have increasing specialisation of brain cells, so that in the end one would be only active, and committedly exclusively for, let us say, recognition of one's grandmother (Greenfield, 1997). Apart from the physiological problems of trying to work out how a neuron would 'know' your grandmother, it also led to problems arising from cell death. If one is losing large numbers of neurons, as happens each day, then it would be unfortunate for your grandmother if that particular one was extinguished! So, the scenario where one neuron corresponded to any event or object in the outside world does not seem very probable. Moreover, although a brain does have many cells, even these would not necessarily be of a number to cater for every single aspect one happened to encounter in life. Somehow, the brain has to reflect the outside world in another way. There are between ten thousand and a hundred thousand connections from one cell and the next. Hence, with a hundred billion neurons, the enormity of the numbers of connections escalates rapidly. In the cortex alone, if you were to count the connections at a rate of one a second, it would take you thirty two million years. If you then try and calculate the permutations and combinations of these connections, it exceeds the number of particles in the universe.

So, by thinking of connections between neurons and their permutations and combinations, one has enormous flexibility. Moreover, any single cells can participate in any number of groups so that you are not confined to a rigid commitment of one cell to one function. If we look at development, it appears that connections probably are the critical feature in the brain, the distinguishing feature of change as we grow in the first two years of life: it is not so much that more cells, but rather more connections, are being formed. You are probably born, more or less, with all the neurons you are ever going to have, but it is your connections that are growing subsequently and that account for the amazing expansion of the brain. It is the connections that are sculptured to our individual biases, prejudices, memories, fears, hopes, fantasies, and experiences as we go through life. So it is the connections that we ought to think about if we are thinking about the epicentre and the question of the trigger for ensuing various aspects of the outside world. There is no 'hard wiring' as such. Rather chemicals that are released in the brain can influence over relatively rapid time-periods the direction that neurons are going to grow.

But it is not just during development that these miraculous events occur. Consider an experiment in adult owl monkeys (Merzenich *et al.* 1991). The monkey subject had to do something very subtle, perform a task with two of its five digits (see Figure 2). So two digits were active at the expense of the others, rotating a little disk. What the researchers looked at was how much area of the relevant part of the brain was allocated to each digit before and after this task; they found that after stimulation there was a clear expansion of the original boundary of the neuronal allocation of relevant digits. Even in adult brains, rather reassuringly, these triggering brain areas will change connections all the time, albeit over seconds or minutes. Therefore, I would like to suggest that the epicentre under discussion, the stone in the puddle, is in fact a *network* of neurons, a group of cells that connected up to each other in the fairly long term. The term 'hard wired' is hardly appropriate, because we have just seen that connections can change according to chemicals that might be available. A current configuration of connections would be activated, for example in a simple sense, if you saw something, although you would not yet be conscious. In any event, we can envisage a hub of cells, corresponding to the stick in the candyfloss, or the stone in the puddle – whatever metaphor seems most helpful. So much for the boss. But what we are really interested in, in a model of consciousness, is how this boss subsequently recruits a group of

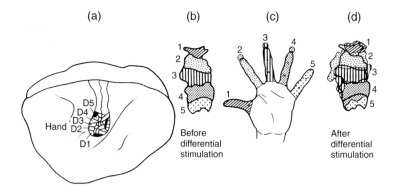

Figure 2 Effects of differential stimulation of two digits in the monkey
Source: E. Kandel and R. D. Hawkin, *Mind and Brain* (W. H. Freeman, 1993) in Greenfield 1997

managers or sub-managers *transiently*. How does activation of a hub of neurons in this way, which in itself does not cause consciousness, is not associated with consciousness – how does it manage to corral or recruit enough neurons that can be associated with appreciable consciousness? One of the fascinating aspects of our minds is that they change all the time: one can look at a cup of tea and view it in a certain way yet a few minutes later you will see it in a different context, a different consciousness. Although it stretches the analogy, imagine the boss going into the office and trying to telephone the managers and sub-managers: but some of them are out to lunch, some of them cannot be bothered to pick up the telephone, some of them have got hangovers and take a long time to pick up the telephone, some of them are staring out of the window, some of them are desperate to talk to the boss and are really waiting by the telephone immediately to pick it up at the first ring. One can imagine that the targets of these telephone calls, different people, are differentially sensitive to recruitment, to being in this telephoning network. So what, in neuronal terms, could be the equivalent? How could we build into the model some way of modulating the sensitivity or the willingness of the neurons to be recruited into an evanescent, large group? Once this feature can be built in to modulating the neurons, then that would give us a basis for both recruiting the neurons at any one time, and indeed varying that recruitment.

Increasingly, people are realising that instead of there being, as computer models would have, just one-to-one local connections, brain chemicals do more than transmit signals within local circuits (Woolf 1996). Increasingly neuroscientists are placing importance on the fact that there appear to be kinds of chemical fountains in the brain. They send projections in a different way to very large areas of the brain, even though the neurons or origins themselves are relatively small. The chemical that is released from these fountains could in some way change the excitability of the cells, namely the willingness to be recruited, or in neuroscientific terms, sensitivity to stimulation. There are now many examples of how the sensitivity of cells' electrical responses can vary to a given stimulation. The important difference is if they are 'modulated' by one of the chemicals released from the fountain. Once the modulating transmitter wears off, the response of the cell reverts back to normal again. The very rapid modulation of the sensitivity of the cells to stimulation is not long term, but rather very transient. There are several different 'modulating fountains' that emanate in different ways out of very large areas of the brain: dopamine, noradrenaline, serotonin and histamine. It is these chemicals that are targeted by anti-depressant drugs and indeed many other mood-modifying substances, such as LSD. So it seems that these chemicals might play an important part in modulating the recruitment of neurons. Also, we know that whether or not you are taking drugs, these chemicals will change during the day. Your bio-rhythms will have different types of these fountains dominating at different times (Hobson 1994). Similarly, in dreams, different chemicals will be dominating. These fountains, then, are very important if we are going to try and understand the physical basis of the mind, indeed, of consciousness (see Figure 3).

CENTRAL PATHWAYS FOR NOREPINEPHRINE, DOPAMINE,
5-HYDROXYTRYPTAMINE, AND HISTAMINE

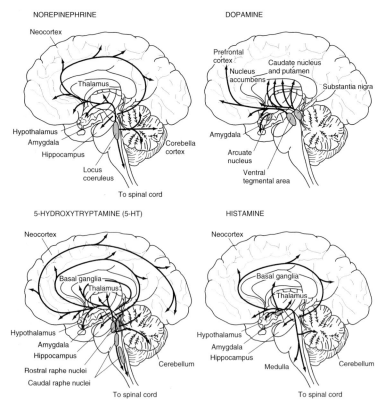

Figure 3 Distribution of amines in the human brain

Source: J. G. Nicholls, A. R. Martin and B. G. Wallace, *From Neuron to Brain* (Sinauer Assocs Inc., 1992)

What evidence is there that evanescent, large groups of cells are formed in the brain? Let us look at two experimental results, one from the frog brain and one from humans which, although they do not directly prove that you have transient formation or neural assemblies associated with consciousness, nonetheless, I think, indicate that it might be plausible. The first experiment was in the frog, done in Israel by Aertsen and his group. These scientists exploited a phenomenon that could not be used in humans because it would mean exposing the brain: they used a special dye that actually changes, fluoresced, according to the excitability of the cell. These so-called 'voltage sensitive dyes' allow us to look at very large groups of brain cells lighting up all at once. Literally, what they did in a very simple experiment was to shine a light at this frog and see how many neurons lit up. One might predict, according to the dicta of conventional neuroscience, that once activated, a group of cells light up, and that is the end of the story – that is our hub. But the results were far more interesting. At the beginning, only a relatively few cells seemed active, but over a period of about half a second, 500 milliseconds, there was a progressive growth of the number of neurons that were gradually recruited around, in this case, the epicentre of the light. Moreover, it is possible to manipulate the extent to which neurons are recruited to a light stimulus, under various conditions. Here neurons do not merely respond to a light in a one-off fashion, but rather grow in extent in their communications like a cloud, like the candyfloss, like ripples from a stone, over time.

Of course, these experiments have been in the frog. How do we know that such phenomena could actually occur with consciousness, and with people? A different type of experiment has been performed with human subjects. Benjamin Libet (Libet 1993) on the West Coast did the following experiment: he took human subjects and simply pricked their skin while recording their brain waves from electrodes attached to the outside of their scalp. Libet then recorded an electrical wave from the part of the brain that receives the most direct connection from nerves coming up the spinal cord: the sharp response he saw within 100 milliseconds could be regarded as the equivalent of the stone in the puddle. The subject did not report consciousness at all. However, over a longer period, of about 500 milliseconds, there was a gradual spreading of the activity over far greater areas of the surface of the brain (see Figure 4). Only when a larger amount of the surface had been activated, again after about half a second the person reported that they felt 'a tingle', and they actually backdated it to then. This experiment is very important

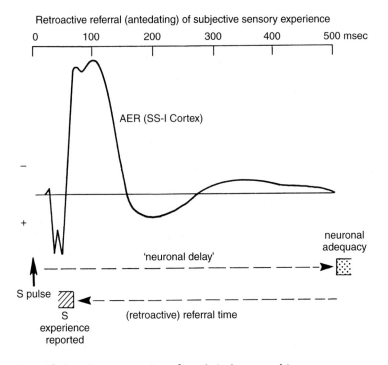

Figure 4 Conscious perception of touch in human subjects
Source: Libet (1993)

because it shows that just because your brain registers a stimulus, it does not mean to say you are conscious of it; but it does mean also that over a longer period it could be that your neurons are building up and slowly recruiting themselves, and that is when one is conscious.

How far can we go with the model as it now stands? An interim conclusion might be that there is no magic ingredient in the brain that can be associated with consciousness: there is no kind of water into wine conversion, no special qualitative factor. If it is not qualitative, consciousness can be more readily explained by being a quantitative phenomenon, where the extent of a transient neuronal assembly could at any one time determine the extent of your consciousness. So let us put this idea to work. In a way those of us exploring the mortal soul are seeking a Rosetta stone. What we want to do is to be able to interpret physiological events in the brain in terms of phenomenology, in terms of the first person, personal world. We also need to go the other way and take a first person, personal experience, and be able to see in it a physical basis. Once we can do that, although we have not established a causality of how the brain generates consciousness, it would be going quite a long way towards at least understanding how the brain does relate to the phenomenology. Let us take a few tentative steps to see how far we might progress, starting with the physiology.

Various factors will determine the size of neuronal assembly. The first factor will be how strong is the triggering epicentre. Is it a very bright light, or is it a very faint light that you can hardly see? The next issue is: how extensive are these neuronal connections? The more extensive they are, then the more subjectively powerful or 'significant' it will be. Finally what is the availability of certain modulatory chemicals? Here three prime factors are: strength of stimulation, degree of connectivity and significance of the epicentre. Scientists often like to explore a scenario by starting with a caricature. Let us imagine the abnormally small neuronal assemblies which could be caused by a modest connectivity, a weak epicentre, or high arousal or hyperactivity, where the chance for a group to grow is curtailed because something else comes along that distracts you and acts as the epicentre for a rival assembly.

In real life could we identify situations in the outside world corresponding to these factors? Let us start with an abnormally weak epicentre. When one is asleep and dreaming, then there is hardly any stimulation from the outside world. When one is dreaming it is a fascinating fact that the brain waves recorded by the EEG reverts to being virtually indistinguishable from when you are awake. It is possible therefore that dreaming consciousness is at the far end of the continuum: it constitutes vestigial neuronal assemblies. Witness the dramatic shift from one scene to another, where suddenly you are in one place and then you are somewhere else, and where things do not have a very strict time or space frame of reference. Perhaps the consciousness of dreaming is the almost random formation of little groups forming in different configurations like pebbles thrown very gently into water. One can imagine the gentle ripples easily being displaced by the next pebble as it hits the water. I would like to suggest that the dreaming consciousness is not *qualitatively* different from ordinary consciousness – rather it is just an extreme example of one that *quantitatively* can be placed at the far end of the spectrum. What if the connections themselves were modest? If one compares the neonatal brain with that of the six-year-old brain, one can see far more connectivity between neurons in the older child

119

(see Figure 5). As regards children's consciousness, a toy may be the epicentre of a child's world, but as soon as it is physically not there, the child is distracted by something else in the environment: he no longer is interested, probably not aware that the toy continues to exist. A small child is only aware of what his senses are telling him. There are not enough inner cerebral resources in the generation of thoughts, for this little toy to still be the centre of his consciousness. It is very interesting that at about 26 weeks *in utero*, the EEG of the foetus is entirely that associated with dreaming sleep (Hobson 1994). During the first year of life it is significantly greater. A one-year-old child spends much more time, has consciousness in dreams, than compared to us crusty older people, who have relatively little percentage of our lives spent in dreams. There is then a progressive decrease in the amount of dreaming time that the brain has, which I would suggest fits in with the idea that it is moderated by a small neuronal assembly state. As your brain becomes more sophisticated the connections become more established, such that it resorts less frequently to the smallest end of consciousness, that of dreams. What about the final contributing factor, arousal and hyperactivity? Here I would like to suggest that when you are highly aroused you

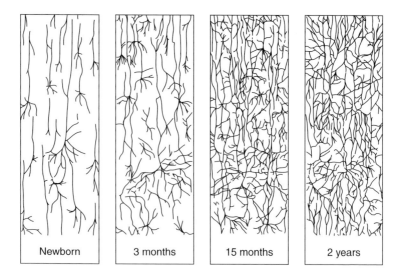

Newborn   3 months   15 months   2 years

Figure 5 Increasing connectivity between brain cells in early stages of development

Source: J. L. Conel, *The Post-Natal Development of the Human Cerebral Cortex*, i (Harvard University Press, 1939), In Greenfield (1997)

are moving around a lot, and therefore encountering more potential triggers, more things in your environment that you are looking at. Hence it will be easier to recruit competing neuronal assemblies which will automatically be small because there will be a high turnover. In addition, perhaps, high arousal, which is associated with certain chemicals, such as dopamine, might not be so good at modulating large neuronal groupings. If one was accepting that, one could say that the phenomonological profile of a small neuronal assembly would be that a raw, sensory consciousness would dominate. You would be very much the victim of your environment, just as a child is. We all know that children, for example, if they cry, can often be pacified with a bar of chocolate. You do not have to reason with a child; whereas if a grown-up cries, a bar of chocolate is probably not going to be a very effective way of alleviating their condition. You are very much the passive recipient of sensory input. I would suggest that in dreams, although the senses are not coming in directly via the sensory organs systems, the relays within the sensory system can be activated by internal brain circuits. One of the features of dreams is that one is very much the passive recipient. One is out of control, things are just happening to you all the time, closing in, and out of context. Similarly children cannot put things in the right context. My brother, for example, when he was very young thought there was a dragon under the bath, and as much as one could logically reassure him that there should be no dragon under the bath, he remained unconvinced. Children, rather like ourselves in our dreaming states, are incapable of rationalising fears and coping with implosions of sensory stimuli. Similarly, for a victim of the outside world, with no inner continuity, there would be abrupt shifts in awareness.

Does this profile occur at all in human beings? I would like to suggest that it could well do so in schizophrenia: schizophrenics are abnormally distracted, or obsessed with the environment. They often see the outside world in glowing colours, which is why sometimes they have illusions that they have special powers (Frith 1992). They are not very good at continuous or logical reasoning, and they are very much the victims of the imploding outside world which they cannot counteract by rational thought and argument. So perhaps schizophrenia is another case where one could say there were small neuronal assemblies.

If one accepts that, then what about large neuronal assemblies? Could we think of a profile, going from physiology to phenomenology, where instead of the sensory world dominating, abstract thought would overpower the outside world which subsequently would seem very remote. In addition, one probably would not be moving around much because one was in an inner world with a strong continuity of thought. Is there any situation we can think of, in caricature terms, that is like that? Clinical depressives, as it happens, quite often see the world as grey and remote. They say people seem a long way off; there are no bright colours. Depressives do not move around much, but persist in the same train of thought all the time, or there is a chilling continuity of logic right through to the conclusion that they might as well die.

Having considered these extreme examples, it would be possible to manipulate each of these factors of neuronal connectivity epicentre, to estimate the consequent size of the neuronal assembly, arousal levels, and assembly turnover, and hence the resulting kind of consciousness. Obviously I have taken extreme examples here because one always, when starting off, is dealing in a sense in caricatures. As we have seen, brains would be dominated by small assemblies because of very sparse connectivity, but despite a strong epicentre: brains would be dominated by dreaming, however there would be extensive connectivity, yet this time a very weak non-sensory epicentre. In schizophrenia there might be normal connectivity, a strong epicentre, yet something aberrant with the fountains of modulating chemicals. Arousal levels are different, and again you have competing assemblies so they are very small.

Incidentally, people who suffer accidents might be similar to those with a tendency for small assembly formation, such as children. People often recount that, when having accidents, events move very slowly. One is very much a victim of the outside world, obviously not dwelling on inner thoughts, but very much the passive recipient of the sensory world. By contrast, abstract thought would entail a medium level of arousal but with extensive connectivity. Finally, Alzheimer's disease again is a situation, sadly, where we have sparse connectivity. The very tragic decrease in the conscious state of Alzheimer patients might be again on a continuum, a shift towards a reduction in degree of consciousness.

What about the other way round: could we travel from phenomenology of everyday life to physiology? Can we think of certain sensations we could then interpret in terms of neuronal assembly size? You might think we all feel the same pain to the same extent all the time, but that is not the case. Interestingly, pain is not constant. When volunteers received electric shocks or cold stimulus through their teeth, the 'threshold' of when it was painful was plotted out throughout the day. Surprisingly in the early morning and late at night it did not take very much stimulation to experience pain, whereas in the middle of the day, more stimulus was needed before the sensation of pain was reported (see Figure 6).

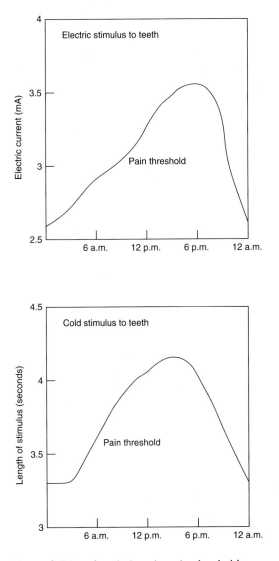

Figure 6 Diurnal variations in pain threshold

Source: J. Burne, J. Farndon, and S. Parker, *The Human Mind* (Marshall Editions Developments Ltd, 1996)

These results immediately throw an interesting light on the *subjective* sensation of pain. One's nerves are not varying, but something is changing in the brain to change the perception of pain. We also know that pain is metaphorical. We all talk of pain in terms of other things, it is 'burning', or 'pricking', or 'stabbing' which suggests that it could be expressed in terms of degree of recruitment of cells because we are seeing it associated with something else. Pain is variable as we have just seen, and is absent in dreams. In morphine analgesia, interestingly enough, apparently the pain is there but it no longer matters any more. It is not so much that it is like an anaesthetic: it does not take the pain away, but rather takes away the *significance* of pain. Perhaps morphine is restricting the formation of the neuronal assemblies. Finally, phantom limb pain in amputees has no obvious source of pain. I would suggest that, in the amputees' case, an obsolete neuronal assembly is present that when active is extensive enough for pain sensation. So, could extent of pain be related to the extent of neuronal assembly?

In summary, I suggest that there is no magic ingredient for consciousness: the critical factor in the brain is not some special qualitative magic bullet that some lucky neuroscientist is going to eventually unearth. Rather, the issue is a quantitative one, depending on the degree of recruitment of neurons: the extent of recruitment will determine your consciousness at any one time from one moment to the next. A true scientist would immediately seek how one was going to test the hypothesis. So, what chance is there of actually proving the model? Once we can obtain a high resolution in human brain imaging, similar to that with invasive techniques in animals, we will be able to test out this idea and develop it. It is only a matter of time, for imaging techniques are improving at an awesome rate. It is a big step for scientists to start to theorise about the modern soul, the mortal soul, consciousness and the mind. Hard experimental data may be just around the corner.

References

Churchland, P.M. (1995) *The Engine of Reason, the Seat of the Soul: A philosophical journey into the brain*, MIT Press

Crick, F. (1994) *The Astonishing Hypothesis* Charles Scribner's Sons

Frith, N.J. (1992) *The Cognitive Neuropsychology of Schizophrenia*, Hillsdale, NJ: Laurence Erlbaum Assocs.

Greenfield, S. A. (1997) *The Human Brain: A Guided Tour*, London: Weidenfeld & Nicholson.

Hobson, A. (1994) *The Chemistry of Curious States: How the Brain Changes its Mind*, Boston: Little, Brown & Co.

Libet, B. (1993) *Neurophysiology of Consciousness*, Boston: Birkauser.

Merzenich *et al.* (1991) 'Reorganization of somatosensory area 3b representations in adult owl monkeys after digital syndactyly', *J Neurophysiology* 63(3): 1048–58.

Posner, M. L. and Raichle, M. E. (1994) *Images of Mind*, Scientific American Library, New York: W. H. Freeman.

Woolf, N. J. (1996) 'Global and serial neurons form a hierarchically arranged interface proposed to underlie memory and cognition', *Neurosci* 74: 625–51.

8

THE SENSE OF THE SELF

Galen Strawson

1   It has been said that human life is founded on three fundamental (and connected) illusions: the illusion of romantic love, the
illusion of free will, and the illusion of the self. This is a rather
sweeping remark: human societies and individuals vary greatly in
their preoccupations, and individuals change their views as they
grow older. But it has a certain force; it's not just a Western view.

Of the three supposed illusions, love is probably the most common
target of scepticism. I'm not going to consider it here, but I think
it may be in better shape than the other two. A thing may be rare
but real, and romantic love is certainly naturalistically respectable:
there is nothing in the theory of evolution that puts it in doubt.

I hold out no hope for free will. It's true that there are many senses
of the word 'free', and in some of these senses we can indeed be said
to have free will. But free will is probably an illusion in the strong
form in which many suppose it to exist. I'm not going to discuss it
here, except to make two brief and connected comments in relation
to Susan Greenfield's chapter. The first is that you don't need to
believe in free will in order to believe in an immortal or immaterial
soul. The second is that you don't need to believe that the mind can
exist without the brain in order to believe in immortal life. On these
points I find I'm backed up by Calvin, St Augustine, and Origen,
the third–century Church Father – not to mention Joseph Priestley,
the great eighteenth–century chemist and devout Unitarian, who
argued powerfully that belief in an immaterial soul was unorthodox
from the Christian point of view.

The self is the most difficult of the three topics. This is partly
because it's so much less clear what we're talking about when we
talk about the self. But I don't think that this is because language
is a special agent of confusion. It's not that the 'seas of language
. . . run . . . high', as Wittgenstein said (1953: §194). Or rather,

they do run high, but the swell is inherent in our experience prior to the attempt to analyse it in language. There is undoubtedly such a thing as the *sense* of the self, even if there is no such thing as the self. I believe that we have to analyse the sense of the self before we can take on the question whether the self exists.

It's true that the phrase 'the self' is very unnatural in most speech contexts in most languages, and some conclude from this that it's an illusion to think that there is such a thing as the self, an illusion that arises from an improper use of language. I think, however, that this is implausible. On this point I disagree with Sir Anthony Kenny. I don't think the problem of the self arises from an unnatural use of language which itself arises from nowhere. Rather, I think that use of a phrase like 'the self' arises from a prior and independent sense that there is such a thing as the self. The phrase may be unusual in ordinary speech, and it may have no obvious direct translation in many languages, but all languages have words that lend themselves naturally to playing the role that 'the self' plays in English, however murky that role may be, and the phrase certainly means something to most people. It has a natural use in religious, philosophical, and psychological contexts, which are very natural contexts of discussion for human beings.

2   I'll devote a few words to this philosophers' dispute before going on with the main argument. Some will reply to me as follows. 'Look: the way we normally use words in communication with each other reveals the true, philosophically unwarped structure of our thought, and in ordinary talk the use of the word 'I' to refer (or apparently refer) to the supposed mental self doesn't stand out as distinct from use of 'I' to refer to the human being considered as a whole. This shows that we cannot properly draw such a distinction, and are talking a kind of nonsense when we try to do so. So the supposed problem of the self arises from an elementary confusion. We can prove that *my # self*, the putative mental self, is either nothing at all, or it is simply *myself*, the living, embodied, publicly observable human being considered as a whole. For the term ('I') that allegedly refers to the former thing undoubtedly refers to the latter thing; so the former thing does not exist separately from the latter thing; so either it is the latter thing, or it is nothing at all (cf. Kenny, 1988:4).'

I think that this argument has no force, and that the appeal to ordinary public language use, in the attempt to solve a philosophical problem, is nowhere more spectacularly inappropriate than in the case of the problem of the self – precisely because such language use standardly reflects the public perspective on things. It is true that referring terms like 'I' (not to mention 'you', 'he' and 'she') are rarely used in ordinary speech in such a way as to reflect any distinction between the putative mental self and the embodied human being considered as a whole. But what does this prove? All it proves is that the public, third-personal (non-first-personal) perspective on things is built into the everyday public use of language. And what does this fact about the everyday public use of language prove about the nature of reality and the scope of intelligible thought? Nothing. It may be true that the best thing to say, in the end, is that there is no such thing as the self, considered as something distinct from the human being, but this is certainly not the right way to try to show that it is true. Even if referring terms like 'I' were *never* used in ordinary communication in a way that indicated awareness or acceptance of a distinction between mental self and embodied human being, this would have no consequences for the question whether or not there is such a thing as the self.

I say 'even if' because the argument fails even on its own terms: the distinction between 'I' the mental self and 'I' the human being is in fact clearly marked in ordinary thought and talk.[1] People naturally and sincerely report certain experiences to each other by saying things like 'I felt completely detached from my body', or 'I felt I was floating out of my body, and looking down on it from above'. Experiences of this sort are particularly vivid and common in adolescence, occurring spontaneously in about 1 in 300 cases; they are not found only in cases of drug-taking or medical extremity. The fact that such floatings and detachings do not actually happen is unimportant. What matters is that there are experiences of this sort, and that statements of the sort just recorded are natural forms of talk about real experiences in which the intended reference of 'I' is not the human being considered as a whole. There is plainly no difficulty – no problem of communication stemming specifically from the use of 'I' – in using language in this way to describe one's experiences to others.

It is true that when we listen to another person's report of such an experience, we naturally take it to be about the whole human being in front of us (or at the other end of the telephone connection), rather than about some separate inner mental entity. This is a deep fact about the way in which we (almost) always relate to each other, experientially, in such communicative situations. But it does not change the fact that the distinction between the use of 'I' to refer to the mental self or someone and the use of 'I' to refer to the embodied human being is clearly and sharply marked in ordinary thought and talk, in such a way that the 'grammatical' or ordinary-language argument of the nonexistence of the problem of the self fails on its own terms.[2]

It seems to me, in fact, that the central or fundamental way in which we (or very many of us) experience ourselves is a mental entity – sex addicts, athletes and supermodels included.[3] Many philosophers and psychologists now find this hard to see (or remember), given recent training fashions in their disciplines, but it is, in large part, a simple consequence of the way in which our mental properties occupy – and tend to dominate – the foreground, when it comes to our apprehension of ourselves. It is not only that we are often preoccupied with our own thoughts and experiences, living with ourselves principally in our inward mental scene, incessantly presented to ourselves as things engaged in mental business.[4] It is also that mental goings on are always and necessarily present, even when we are thoroughly preoccupied with our bodies, or, generally, with things in the world other than our own mental goings on. Obviously we can be the subjects of mental goings on without being explicitly aware of them as such. Our attention can be intensely focused outward. But even then we tend to have a constant background awareness of our own mental goings on – it is usually inadequate to say that it is merely background awareness – and a constant tendency to flip back to some explicit sense of ourselves as minded or conscious.

It has, as remarked, become hard for philosophers and psychologists then to give these facts their proper weight. Many of them are extraordinarily anxious to dissociate themselves from a view they call 'Cartesianism', when discussing the nature of mind. In consequence, they tend to throw out everything that is right about 'Cartesianism' along with anything that is wrong. In the present context of discussion, they tend to lay very heavy stress on our constant background awareness of our bodies. But this awareness is fully compatible with our thinking of ourselves primarily or centrally as mental things; and those who stress somatic awareness risk forgetting that it is just as true to say that there is constant background (as well as foreground) awareness of our minds. Kinaesthetic experience and other forms of proprioceptive experience of body are just that – experience – and in so far as they contribute constantly to our overall sense of ourselves, they not only contribute awareness of the body, they also contribute themselves together with background awareness of themselves. The notion of background awareness is imprecise, but it seems plausible to say that there is certainly never *less* background awareness of awareness (i.e. of mind) than there is background awareness of body.

To say that the central way in which we conceive of ourselves is as a mental thing is not to say that we are right or wise to do so. Nor is to deny that we also have a strong natural tendency to think of ourselves as Strawsonian persons, essentially unified single things to which mental and non-mental predicates are equally and equally fundamentally applicable: human beings considered as a whole.[5] Nor is it to deny that the primary way in which we ordinarily think of people *other* than ourselves is as Strawsonian persons, human beings considered as a whole. The fact remains that a dualism of conception that distinguishes between the person as mental thing and the person as non-mental thing goes to the very bottom of our thought; especially when we are concerned with ourselves. It is arguable that it *tends* always, and powerfully, towards a conception of the body and the self as somehow distinct entities, even though it coexists comfortably, in the normal course of things, with an equally natural tendency to conceive of people (including oneself) as essentially unified, single things; human beings considered as a whole.

The second conception of persons – the Strawsonian conception of them as unified human beings – is stamped deep into our ordinary apprehension of others and our normal use of language in communication, but it is not similarly stamped into our fundamental use of language in private thought. There are no easy or guaranteed inferences from facts about ordinary public language use to facts about how we fundamentally – or really – think about things. (Psychology is not that easy.) Nor do facts about public language use prove that self-experience involves an illusion. (Metaphysics is not that easy.) And when we think in private, nothing stops us from doing what we (or very many of us) naturally do: which is, to think of ourselves as, primarily or fundamentally, mental things.[6] Facts about ordinary public language use cannot break in our inner privacy and tell us that we are not really doing what we think we are doing (not really thinking what we think we are thinking).

Let us now return to the main argument.

3   Human beings in different cultures are much more alike, psychologically speaking, than most present-day anthropologists and sociologists suppose. There's a great deal of detailed and complex

substance to the idea of a common humanity – to the idea that there are profound emotional and cognitive similarities between human beings that wholly transcend differences in cultural experience. It's also true that human beings are very varied, psychologically; but it's arguable that the deepest and most important psychological differences between human beings are those that can be found within any given culture, rather than those that are apparent when one compares different cultures. I think it's no exaggeration to say that the cultural relativism of Emile Durkheim and others, which has been elegantly renewed by Clifford Geertz, and which is orthodox in large parts of the academic community, has been severely undermined by recent work in the discipline now known as evolutionary psychology. It is based on an underestimation of the genetic determinants of human nature, and a false view about human mental development.[7]

It's partly for this reason, and partly because I have a Kantian confidence in the ability of philosophy to reach conclusions of extreme generality in this area, that I expect my remarks about the self to apply, if true, to human beings generally, and perhaps to any being that can be said to have a sense of the self. In so far as human variations in the sense of the self will be of concern, they are variations that can be found within particular cultures, not variations that result from differences of culture. When it comes to the sense of the self, the difference between those who can't sleep and those who can may be more important than any cultural differences.

My doubts about the extent to which the fundamentals of human psychology are affected by culture make me a 'humanist', in a fairly new sense of the term. There exists, today, an influential academic culture in which the word 'humanist' is an insult, but it's still hard to imagine that it's not a nice thing to be.

4   So what do I mean by the sense of the self? I don't mean the kind of thing that is discussed in books about 'personal growth'. I mean the sense that people have of themselves as being, specifically, a mental presence; a mental someone; a single mental thing that is a conscious subject, that has a certain character or personality, and that is distinct from all its particular experiences, thoughts, hopes, wishes, feelings, and so on. I'll mark this by talking of the *mental* self.

I have no doubt that such a sense of the mental self comes to every normal human being, in some form, in childhood. The early realization of the fact that one's thoughts are unobservable by others, the experience of the profound sense in which one is alone in one's head, these are among the very deepest facts about the character of human life, and found the sense of the mental self. It is perhaps most often vivid when one is alone and thinking, but it can be equally vivid in a room full of people. It connects with a feeling that nearly everyone has had intensely at some time – the feeling that one's body is just a vehicle or vessel for the mental thing that is what one really or most essentially is.[8] As remarked, I think there is a sense in which this is the central or primary way in which we think of ourselves, although some analytic philosophers may find this hard to see.

I'm not claiming that the sense of the mental self automatically incorporates some sort of belief in an immaterial soul, or in life after bodily death. It doesn't. Philosophical materialists who believe, as I do, that we are wholly physical beings, and that the theory of evolution by natural selection is true, and that consciousness of the sort with which we are familiar evolved by purely physical natural processes on a planet where no such consciousness previously existed, have this sense of the mental self as strongly as anyone else.

5   Let me now expand the initial description. I propose that the mental self is conceived or experienced as (a) a *thing*, in some reasonably robust sense. It is thought of as (b) *mental*, in some sense. It is thought of as *single*, in a way that requires further specification: both when considered (c) at a time and (d) through time. It is thought of as something that is (e) *ontologically distinct* from its thoughts, experiences, and so on, and indeed from all other things. It is thought of as something that is (f) a *subject of experience*, a conscious feeler, thinker, chooser, decider, it is thought of as (g) an *agent*, and it is thought of as something that has a certain character or (h) *personality*. This list may be too full, but it provides a base and a target, and I'll say a little more about each of the elements before raising the question of whether they are all essential to anything that can be called a sense of the self. In so doing, I'll use the expression 'the (mental) self' freely, but I obviously don't want to exclude in advance the view that there is no such thing, and the expression will often function as a loose name for what one might equally well call 'the self-phenomenon', i.e. all those undoubtedly real phenomena of experience that lead us to think and talk in terms of something called the self, whether or not there is such a thing.

(a)   The self is thought of as a thing.   In a way, this is the least clear of the eight claims, but the general idea is this: the self is not

thought of as a state or property of something else, or as an event, or as a mere process or series of events. So, in a sense, there is nothing else for it to seem to be, other than a thing. It's not thought of as being a thing in the way that a stone or a chair is, but it is none the less thought of as a thing of some kind. It is, in particular, thought of as something that has the typical causal profile of a thing – as something that can *undergo* things and *do* things. I think Bishop Berkeley's characterization of the self as a 'thinking active principle' is as good as any, when one is trying to characterize the way in which the self is thought of as a thing. A principle, in this old use, manages to sound like a thing of some sort without sounding anything like a table or a chair.

The question 'What is a thing?' is very difficult and needs further discussion. But this will have to do for the moment.

(b)   The self is thought of as something mental.   This claim is also unclear, but the idea is something like this: when the self is thought of as a thing, a 'thinking principle', it is thought of as being a thing specifically in so far as it is a mental phenomenon. That is, its claim to thinghood is thought of as being sufficiently grounded in its mental nature alone. It may also *have* a non-mental nature (as materialists suppose), but its counting as a thing is not thought to depend on its counting as a thing when considered in its non-mental nature. The self is the *mental* self. It is taken to be a thing or entity just as something mental.

Once again, the claim is not that the ordinary sense of the mental self necessarily incorporates some sort of belief in an immaterial soul. It doesn't. The fact remains that the self is thought of as a specifically mental entity. It's true and important that people also naturally think of themselves as living human beings that essentially possess both mental and non-mental properties. But this doesn't affect the present point about how the mental self is standardly conceived.

Although experience of the mental self needn't involve any belief in an immaterial soul, it does incorporate elements that make that belief come rather naturally to human beings. Experientially speaking, the mental self can easily seem to exist, and to exist self-sufficiently, in a sphere of being that is quite other than the sphere of being described by physics. Things are not as they seem, according to materialists. But they certainly seem as they seem. And this helps to explain how natural it is for us to think of the self as a specifically mental thing.

(c, d) The self is thought of as single. Clearly, to think of the self as a thing is already to think of it as single in some way – as *a* thing. But in what way? I have three main claims in mind.

First: in so far as the mental self is thought of as single, it is not thought of as having singularity only in the sense in which a group of things can be said to be a single group. Rather it is thought of as single in the way in which a single marble (e.g.) is single when compared with a single pile of marbles.

Second: the mental self's property of singleness is thought of as sufficiently and essentially grounded in its mental nature alone, just as the self's claim to thinghood is thought of as sufficiently grounded in its mental nature alone. The mental self may *have* a (non-mental) nature in addition to a mental nature, and it may be believed (by the being whose experience or conception of self is in question) to have a non-mental nature. But its counting as single is not thought of as depending on its counting as single when considered in its non-mental nature – as a single brain, say. It is taken to be single just as something mental.

Third: the mental self is standardly thought to be single both when it is considered synchronically, or as a thing existing at a given time, and when it is considered diachronically, i.e. as a thing that persists through time. I'm going to stretch the meaning of the word 'synchronic' slightly, and take it to apply to any consideration of the mental self (or self-phenomenon) that is a consideration of it during an *experientially unitary* or *hiatus-free* period of thought or experience. 'Diachronic' will accordingly apply to any consideration of the mental self (or self-phenomenon) during any period of conscious thought or experience that includes a break or hiatus.

I'll expand on this notion of a hiatus or gap later. For the moment I'll simply assert that in the normal course of events truly hiatus-free periods of thought or experience are invariably brief in human beings: a few seconds at the most, a fraction of a second at the least. Our eyes are constantly engaged in saccadic jumps, and reflection reveals the respect in which our minds function in an analogous – if more perceptible – way. Research by Pöppel and others provides 'clear evidence that . . . the experienced Now is not a point, but is extended', and 'that the [human] conscious Now is – language and culture independent – of the duration of approximately 3 seconds'. By itself this proves nothing about the existence of hiatuses, or about the nature of the self, but it is undeniably suggestive (Ruhnau 1995: 168; Pöppel 1978). Citing this research in his essay 'The Dimension of the Present Moment', the Czech immunologist and poet Miroslav Holub writes that 'in this sense our ego lasts three seconds' (1990: 6).

I've said that human beings standardly have a sense of the singleness of the mental self. But some may claim to experience the mental self as fragmentary or multiple, and most of us have had experience that gives us – so we feel – some understanding of what they mean.

It seems, however, that the experience of multiplicity can at most affect (*d*), the sense of the mental self as diachronically single (recall that a sense of the mental self as diachronically single may well be concerned with short periods of time; when I want to consider longer periods of time – weeks, years, lifetimes – I will talk about 'long-term' continuity). It cannot affect (*c*), the sense of the mental self as synchronically single (single during any one 'hiatus-free' period of thought or experience). Why not? Because any candidate for being an experience of the mental self as synchronically multiple at the present moment will have to be an episode of explicitly self-conscious thought, and there is a crucial (trivial) respect in which no such episode could be experience of the mental self as synchronically multiple. Explicitly self-conscious thought need not always involve some explicit sense of the mental self as something present and involved, even when it has the form 'I', or 'I am *F*' ('I forgot the key', 'I'm late for my exam'). But whenever it does – and it must if there is to be anything that is a candidate for being an *experience* of the mental self as synchronically multiple at the present moment – there is a fundamental respect in which the mental self must be experienced as single, for the space of that thought at least.

This may seem obvious, but it can be disputed. It may be said that even experience of the mental self synchronically considered can seem to be experience of something shattered and multiple ('My name is legion', Mark 5:9). There seem to be forms of human experience that invite such a description. One may be under stress and subject to rapidly changing moods. One may feel oneself pulled in different directions by opposed desires. Human thought-processes can become extraordinarily rapid and tumultuous. But what exactly is being claimed, when it is said that the self may be experienced as synchronically multiple? There seem to be two main possibilities: either the experience is that are many selves present, or it is (just) that the self is complex in a certain radical way. But in the second case, the experience of radical complexity that is claimed to justify the description 'synchronically multiple' clearly depends on a prior sense of the mental self as synchronically single: in this case 'multiple' is a characterization that is applied to something that must have already presented as single in order for the characterization to be applied at all.

What about the first case, in which the experience is that there are many selves present? Well, we may ask who has the experience that there are many selves present. To face the question is to realize that any explicitly self-conscious experience has to present as experience from one single point of view. If so, the experience that there are many selves present is necessarily experience from some single point of view. Even if a single brain is the site of many experiences that there are many selves present, each such experience is necessarily experience from a single point of view. This is the trivial aspect of the claim that experience of the mental self as synchronically multiple is not really possible.

It may be added that when one's mind races and tumbles, it is natural to experience oneself as a largely helpless spectator of the pandemonium. To this extent, experience of chaotic disparateness of contents reinforces a sense of singleness rather than diminishing it. Nor can one experience conflict of desire unless one experiences both desires as one's own.

(e)   The mental self is thought of as ontologically distinct.   No doubt. But from what? The question has various answers. To begin with, the mental self is thought of as ontologically distinct from any conscious mental goings on – thoughts, experiences, and so on. According to the ordinary view, the mental self *has* thoughts, experiences, emotions, and so on, but it is certainly not the same as them. It is not constituted out of them.

This view also has a stronger version, according to which the mental self is not only distinct from any 'occurrent' conscious mental goings on; it is also distinct from any dispositional mental features like beliefs, preferences, memories, character traits, and so on. It *has* beliefs, preferences, character traits, and so on, but it is not the same thing as them. It is not constituted out of them.

David Hume famously challenged the first of these views. According to his 'bundle' theory of the self, the self is *not* ontologically distinct from a series of mental goings on: it just *is* a series of mental goings on – in so far as it can be said to exist at all. Ordinary thought rejects the bundle theory, however, as Hume later did himself, and endorses the second, stronger version of the ontological distinctness view described in the last paragraph.

A third and still stronger version rejects materialism. It claims that the mental self is ontologically distinct from anything physical.

But this dualist or idealist idea is not an integral part of the human sense of the mental self. The ordinary, unreflective experience of the mental self as something distinct from all its mental goings on and dispositions doesn't depend in any way on belief in an immaterial soul, or in the survival of the mind after the death of the body. You can have this experience full strength even if you are an atheistic materialist.

(f) *The mental self is thought of as a subject of experience.* I take this to be obvious. It has already been proposed that the self is naturally thought of as some sort of thing. This prompts the question 'What sort of thing?', and the natural first answer is: 'A subject of experience'. What is a subject of experience? The question requires consideration, but the ordinary notion of a subject of experience seems pretty clear and accurate. As Susan Greenfield points out, each of us has a very good idea of what a subject of experience is just in being one and being self-conscious. And that's all I need.

The mental self is clearly not the only thing that is thought of as a subject of experience. It's just as natural (or more natural) for us to say that human beings considered as a whole are subjects of experience, together with millions of non-human animals. Nevertheless, we also have a tendency to think that in the human case it is above all the mental self that is the subject of experience. It may be that this way of conceiving of the subject of experience comes most strongly to most of us when we are alone and thinking, but whether this is so or not, the idea that it is, in some sense, the mental self alone that is the subject of experience is an essential constituent of our ordinary sense or conception of the mental self.

(g) *The mental self is thought of as an agent.* The word 'subject' has a well-known polarity. On the one hand it has a passive connotation of subjection: subjects of experience are subject *to* experience. They undergo it – the cold, the crimson, the craving, the car alarm – whether they like it or not. On the other hand it has an active connotation: the *subject* of experience or consciousness is standardly thought of as an essentially active thing, an intentional agent, and this idea of agency is clearly part of the ordinary conception of the mental self.

William James insists strongly on the point. The mental self, he says, is thought of as 'the *active* element in all consciousness . . . the source of effort and attention, and the place from which . . . emanate the fiats of the will'; it is the 'central active self'. 'The very core and nucleus of our self, as we know it, the very sanctuary of our life, is the sense of activity which certain inner states possess. The sense of activity is often held to be a direct revelation of the living substance of our Soul' (James 1950: 297–8, 299; 1984: 163). So agenthood certainly earns its place in a general characterization of the ordinary human sense of the mental self, even if it is not necessary to any possible genuine sense of the mental self.

(h)   The mental self is thought of as having character or personality.   In fact it is thought of as having a personality in exactly the same way as a human being considered as a whole is thought of as having a personality. This is hardly surprising, for we take it that a human being's personality is a matter of how he or she is, mentally speaking; so if we think that the existence of a human being involves the existence of a mental self, we're bound to think that the mental self has the personality that the human being has.

5   So much, very rapidly, for the eight proposed components of our sense of the self. All of them deserve further discussion. My present claim is simply that they are what one should start from, when attempting to answer the question: What is the sense of the self?

After one has attempted to answer this question, one gets a new question: is the sense of the self an accurate representation of anything that actually exists? In other words: is there in fact such a thing as the self? I can't answer this question now. But I'm going to try, while continuing to talk about the sense of the self, to do some work towards an answer.

Suppose that the eight elements do capture the conceptual core of the ordinary human sense of the self. The following question then arises: Does anything that can count as a genuine sense of the mental self really have to contain all these elements? Are they all essential? This question is worth investigation, for if something weaker can count as a genuine sense of the self, then it may be easier to argue that there really is such a thing as the self.

I'm going to argue that at least two of the eight elements can go: (*d*), the diachronic singularity element, and (*h*), the personality element. Actually I think that (*g*), the agency component, can also go, but I'm only going to argue against (*d*) and (*h*). I will begin with (*h*), and, like William James, I will sometimes write 'in the first person, leaving my description to be accepted by those to whose introspection it may commend itself as true, and confessing my inability to meet the demands of others, if others there be' (1950: 299).

The principal point is simple. Most people have at some time, and however temporarily, experienced themselves as a kind of bare locus of consciousness not just as detached, but as void of personality, stripped of particularity of character, a mere point of view. Some have experienced it for long periods of time. This may be the result of exhaustion or solitude, abstract thought or a hot bath. It is also a common feature of severe depression, in which one may experience 'depersonalization'. This is a very accurate term, in my experience and in that of others I have talked to.

Sustained experience of depersonalization is classified as psychotic relative to the normal human condition, but it is of course experientially real, and one can imagine human beings getting stuck in this condition; some do. Equally, one can imagine aliens for whom it is the normal condition. Such an alien may still have a clear sense of the self as a specifically mental thing. It may still have an unimpaired sense of itself as a locus of consciousness, just as we ordinarily do – not only when we suffer depersonalization, but also in everyday life.

A very strong form of what may be lost in depersonalization is recorded by Gerard Manley Hopkins, who talks of considering

> my self-being, my consciousness and feeling of myself, that taste of myself, of *I* and *me* above and in all things, which is more distinctive than the taste of ale or alum, more distinctive than the smell of walnutleaf or camphor, and is incommunicable by any means to another man . . . Nothing else in nature comes near this unspeakable stress of pitch, distinctiveness, and selving, this selfbeing of my own.
> (Hopkins 1959: 123 quoted in Glover 1988: 59)

My enquiries suggest that while some people feel they know exactly what Hopkins means, most find this deeply bewildering: for them, their personality is something that is unnoticed, and in effect undetectable, in the present moment. It's what they look through, or where they look from; not something they look at; a global and invisible condition of their life, like air, not an object of experience. Dramatic differences like these back up the view that we need a phenomenology of the sense of the self before we try to answer the factual question about whether or not there is such a thing as the self.

6 I have suggested that a genuine sense of the self does not require thinking of the self as something that has personality. I am now going to argue that a genuine sense of the self does not require thinking of the self as something that has long-term diachronic singleness, or continuity. I think that a sense of the self may be vivid and complete, at any given time, even if it has to do only with the present, brief hiatus-free stretch of consciousness, at any given time.

It may be said that this is obviously a formal possibility, but that it is remote from reality and from our interests. It may be said that life without any significant sense of the relatively long-term continuity of the mental self is conceivable for aliens, but hardly possible for human beings. Strictly speaking, all I need for my argument is the formal possibility. But it seems to me that life without any sense of the long-term continuity of the mental self does lie well within the range of human experience. One can be fully aware of the fact that one has long-term continuity as a *human being* without ipso facto having any sense of the *mental self* as something that has long-term continuity. One can have a vivid sense of oneself as a mental self, and a strong natural tendency to think that that is what one most truly or fundamentally *is*, while having little interest in or commitment to the idea that the I who is now thinking has any past or future. This idea may have very little – or no – emotional importance for one. It may contribute little or nothing to the overall character of one's experience at any given time.

Perhaps a sustained practice of Buddhist meditation may bring this about. But it may also occur more spontaneously. Human beings differ deeply in a number of ways that may affect their experience of the mental self as something continuous. Some have an excellent 'personal' memory (i.e. memory of their own past life) and an unusual capacity for vivid recollection. Others have a very poor personal memory. And it may not be simply poor. It may also be highly quiescent, and almost never intrude spontaneously into their current thought. These deep differences of memory are matched by equal differences in the force with which people imagine, anticipate, or form intentions about the future.

These differences interact with others. Some people live deeply in narrative mode: they experience their lives in terms of something that has shape and story, narrative trajectory. Some of them are self-narrators in a stronger sense: they regularly rehearse and revise their interpretations of their lives. Some people, again, are great planners, and knit up their lives with long-term projects.

Others are quite different. They have no early ambition, no later sense of vocation, no interest in climbing a career ladder, no tendency to see their life in narrative terms or as constituting a story or a development. Some merely go from one thing to another. They live life in a picaresque or episodic fashion. Some people make few plans and are little concerned with the future. Some live intensely in the present, some are simply aimless.

Many things can encourage or obstruct a sense of the mental self as something that has long-term diachronic continuity. Some people are very consistent in personality or character, whether or not they know it. And this form of steadiness may in some cases strongly underwrite experience of the mental self's continuity. Others are consistent only in their inconsistency, and may for that reason feel themselves to be continually puzzling, and piecemeal. Some go through life as if stunned.

Neither inconsistency nor poor memory is necessary for the episodic experience of life. John Updike has an extremely powerful personal memory and a highly consistent character, and writes, in his autobiography, 'I have the persistent sensation, in my life and art, that I am just beginning' (1989: 239). I believe that this is an accurate description of how things are for many people, when it comes to that sense of oneself as a mental self that is – whether or not it is acknowledged – central to most people's self-conception. My experience is the same as Updike's, and I learn from him that this is nothing essentially to do with my extremely weak personal memory.

I find, then, that I am somewhere down the episodic end of the spectrum. I have no sense of my life as a narrative with form, or indeed as a narrative without form. I have little interest in my own past and little concern for the future. My poor personal memory rarely impinges on my present consciousness. Even when I am interested in my past, I'm not interested in it specifically in so far as it is mine. I'm perfectly well aware that it is mine, in so far as I am a human being considered as a whole, but I do not really think of it as mine at all, in so far as 'mine' picks out me as I am now. For me as I am now, the interest (emotional or otherwise) of my personal memories lies in their experiential content considered independently of the fact that what is remembered happened *to me* – i.e. to the me that is now remembering. They're certainly distinctive in their 'from-the-inside' character, but this in itself doesn't mark them as mine in any emotionally significant sense. The one striking exception to this, in my case, used to be – but no longer is – memory of recent embarrassment.

I make plans for the future. To that extent I think of myself perfectly adequately as something that has long-term continuity. But I experience this way of thinking of myself as utterly remote and theoretical, given the most central or fundamental way in which I think of myself, which is as a mental self or someone. Using 'Me*' to express this fundamental way in which I think of myself – or to denote me thinking of myself in this way, looking out on things from this perspective – I can accurately express my experience by saying that I do not think of Me* as being something in the future. It is also accurate to shift the 'not', and say, more strongly, that what I think of as being in the future is not Me*.

It is January as I write the lecture on which this chapter is based. The thought that I have to give a Wolfson College lecture in March causes me some worry, and this has familiar physiological manifestations. I feel the anxiety naturally and directly as pertaining to me even though I have no sense that it will be Me* that will be giving the lecture. Indeed it seems completely false to say that it will be Me*. And this is how it feels, not something I believe for theoretical reasons. So why do I feel any anxiety now? I believe that susceptibility to this sort of anticipatory anxiety is innate and 'hardwired', a manifestation of the instinct for self-preservation: my practical concern for my future, which I believe to be within the normal human range, is biologically grounded and autonomous in such a way that it persists as something immediately felt even though it is not supported by any emotionally backed sense on the part of Me* now that Me* will be there in the future. (Not even half an hour away, and certainly not tomorrow.) In so far as I have any sense of Me* (rather than the living human being that I am) as something with a history and future, it seems that this sense is a wispy, short-range *product* of, and in no way a *ground* of, my innate predisposition to such forward and backward looking things as anxiety or regret. And it dislimms when scrutinized, and it is more accurate to say that it does not exist.

Now for an exception. You might expect me to say that when I think of my death at some unspecified future time, I think that it is not Me* who is going to die, or at least that I do not think that it is Me*. But I do think that it is Me* that is going to die, and I feel fear of death. It's only when I consider future events *in life* that I do not think it's Me*. This seems odd, given that my death necessarily comes after any future events in my life, and ought therefore to seem to have even less to do with Me* than any future events in life. But it can be explained. This feature of my attitude to death is principally grounded in susceptibility to the following line of thought: When eternity – eternal non-existence – is in question, the gap between Me* and death that is created by the fact that I still have an indefinite amount of life to live approximates to nothing (like any finite number compared with infinity). So death – non-existence for ever – presents itself as having direct relevance for Me* now even if Me* has no clear future in life – not even tomorrow. On the vast scale of things that one naturally thinks in terms of when thinking of death, death is no significant distance away from Me*, and looms as something that will happen to Me*. This is not to say that I feel or fear that I am going to die now. The thought of eternity doesn't override common sense. But it has an emotional force that makes it seem plain that death faces Me*. (If this is Heideggerian authenticity, then Heideggerian authenticity is compatible with lack of any belief in the persisting self.)

Note that this line of thought will have equal force for someone who *does* think of their Me* as having a future in life: for if eternity of non-existence is what you fear, a few years is not a protection. This idea was vivid for me as a young child combining an atheist upbringing with great difficulty in going to sleep.

One indirect lesson of this case is important. It is that one's sense of one's temporal nature may vary considerably depending on what one is thinking about. But the general conclusion I draw is that a sense of the self need not necessarily involve (*d*) a sense of it as something that has long-term continuity.

Someone may say: 'This may be how it is for you, but it's not like this for me, and many will find your claim about the phenomenology of the sense of the mental self to be false, or at best unconvincing. They will suspect that it is the distorted product of a prior theoretical commitment.'

Some may be suspicious, others won't be. There's no escape from the facts of human difference, which cause extraordinary misunderstanding and matching misery. My experience of the mental self is just one kind among others; no doubt some people have it in a more extreme form. It matters here only in so far as it supports the claim that a sense of the mental self need not necessarily involve (*d*), a sense of the mental self as something that has long–term singleness and continuity. (*d*) may be a common component of the human sense of self, but it is not universal, it fades over time in some, and is withered, in others, by reflection.

7   I'm now going to raise a completely different doubt about the idea that a genuine sense of the mental self must be a sense of it as something that has long-term diachronic continuity. In a way, it's a peripheral doubt; but it's also rather interesting.

Some think that conscious experience flows. They think this is a basic phenomenological fact – something that is simply given prior to any theoretical suppositions. According to William James

> Consciousness . . . does not appear to itself chopped up in bits. Such words as 'train' or 'chain' do not describe it fitly as it presents itself in the first instance. It is nothing jointed; it flows. A 'river' or a 'stream' are the metaphors by which it is most naturally described. . . . *[L]et us call it the stream of consciousness, or of subjective life.*
>
> (1984: 145)

This seemed like a good move in 1890, given the dominant psychological atomism that inspired the metaphors of trains and chains, collections, bundles, and heaps. But perhaps we have now been misled in the opposite direction – into thinking that consciousness has a more fluent appearance than it does. The question is worth considering, for if consciousness does feel streamlike then this may be part – although only a part – of the explanation of why many people have a sense of the mental self as something that has long term continuity.

Is the 'stream' of thought a stream? People vary. They may answer along a spectrum from 'Yes' to 'No', via 'Usually', 'Sometimes', and 'Almost never'. But one can't assume their answers are true even if they are sincere. People's surface beliefs about their thought processes may conflict with the way their thought processes appear when considered more carefully. You may feel that your thought processes constitute a stream because you believe they do – rather than believing that they do because they felt like that before you formed any belief about them.

I think the metaphor of the stream is very inept, even though streams contain pools and falls – not to mention weeds and stones. Human thought has very little natural phenomenological continuity or experiential flow, if mine is anything to go by. 'Our thought is fluctuating, uncertain, fleeting', as Hume said (1947: 194). It keeps slipping from mere consciousness into self-consciousness and out again (one can sit through whole film without emerging into I-thinking self-consciousness). It is always shooting off, fuzzing, shorting out, spurting and stalling. William James described it as 'like a bird's life, . . . an alternation of flights and perchings' (1950: 243), but even this recognition that thought is not a matter of even flow retains a strong notion of continuity, in so far as a bird traces a spatio-temporally continuous path. It fails to take adequate account of the fact that trains of thought are constantly broken by detours – byblows – fissures – white noise. This is especially so when one is just sitting and thinking. Things are different if one's attention is engaged by some ordered and continuous process in the world, like a fast and exciting game, or music, or a talk. In this case thought or experience may be felt to inherit much of the ordered continuity of the phenomenon which occupies it. But it may still seize up, fly off, or flash with perfectly extraneous matter from time to time, and reflection reveals gaps and fadings, disappearances and recommencements even when there is stable succession of content. It is arguable that the case of solitary speculative thought – in which the mind is left to its own resources and devices – merely reveals in a relatively dramatic way something that is true to a greater or lesser extent of all thought. There is an important respect in which James Joyce's use of punctuation in his 'stream of consciousness' novel *Ulysses* makes his depiction of the character of the process of consciousness more accurate in the case of the heavily punctuated Stephen Daedalus than in the case of the unpunctuated Molly Bloom. Dorothy Richardson, acknowledged as the inventor of the 'stream of consciousness' novel in English, remarked on the 'perfect imbecility' of the phrase to describe what she did.[9]

My claim is not just that there can be radical disjunction at the level of subject matter. Switches of subject matter could be absolute, and still be seamless in the sense that they involved no sensed temporal gap or felt interruption of consciousness. It seems to me, however, that such experience of temporal seamlessness is rare. When I am alone and thinking I find that my fundamental experience of consciousness is one of *repeated returns into consciousness from a state of complete, if momentary, unconsciousness*. The (invariably brief) periods of true experiential continuity are usually radically disjunct from one another in this way even when they are not radically disjunct in respect of content. (It is in fact often the same thought – or nearly the same thought – that one returns to after a momentary absence.) The situation is best described, it seems to me, by saying that consciousness is continually *restarting*. There isn't a basic substrate (as it were) of continuous consciousness interrupted by various lapses and doglegs. Rather, conscious thought has the character of a (nearly continuous) series of radically disjunct irruptions into consciousness from a basic substrate of non-consciousness. It keeps banging out of nothingness; it is a series of comings to.

As remarked, some hiatuses in the process of consciousness involve complete switches of focus and subject matter. Others occur between thoughts that are connected in subject matter, or when one is attending to something in such a way that one hardly notices the hiatus because the content of experience is more or less the same after the hiatus as before. In this second kind of case the hiatus may be a simple blank, a mere caesura, an entirely accidental feature of the mechanism of consciousness. But it is likely that it is also functional in some way, part of a basic process of regirding one's attention: a necessary reprise, a new cast, a new binding of the mental manifold; a new synthesis in the Kantian sense. The hiatus is often fast: it's not hard to overlook the recurrent flicks and crashes of consciousness, the absolute fugues and interstitial vacancies – just as we overlook the blinks of our eyes. But they are easily noticeable when attended to, available to memory in one's current state of consciousness.

Perhaps this is a rash generalization from my own case, or an unwitting confession of schizophrenia. I think, though, that introspection will reveal the same to everyone, if in different degrees. It's true that belief in the reality of flow may itself contribute to an experience of it. But I think that the appearance of flow is undercut by even a modest amount of reflection.

'But perhaps the experience of disjunction is an artefact of introspection', you say. 'Perhaps unexamined consciousness has true flow, and the facts get distorted by the act of trying to observe what they are.' This seems highly implausible. Awareness of radical disjunction sometimes surfaces spontaneously and unlooked for. We can become aware that this is what has been happening, we do not see it only when we look. This is my experience, at least, and the claim seems strongly supported by work described by Dennett (1991: e.g. ch. 11). And even if the appearance of disjunction were partly an artefact of intentional introspection, this would be a striking fact about how consciousness appears to itself, something one needed to take account of when considering the underpinnings of the sense of the self. There's a respect in which this issue is undecidable, for in order to settle it one would need to be able to observe something while it was unobserved. Nevertheless, the view that there is radical disjunction might receive independent support from experimental psychology, and also, more indirectly, from current work on the non-mental neural correlates of consciousness.

My claim, in any case, is that the sense of the mental self as something that has long-term continuity lacks a certain sort of direct phenomenological warrant in the moment-to-moment nature of our thought processes. It is not supported at the level of detail by any phenomenon of steady flow. If there is any support for belief in the long-term continuity of the self in the nature of moment-to-moment consciousness, it is derived indirectly from other sources – the massive constancies and developmental coherencies of *content* that often link up experiences through time, and by courtesy of short-term memory, across all the jumps and breaks of flow. One (the living human being, the mental-and-non-mental whole) walks from A to B, looking around, thinking of this and that. One works in a room for an hour. One looks up at the rain on the window and turns back to the page. One holds the same pen throughout. One is lost in thought, with no conscious awareness of one's body. Examined in detail, the processes of one's thought may be bitty and scatty in the way described; consciousness is 'in a perpetual flux', in Hume's words, and different thoughts and experiences 'succeed each other with an inconceivable rapidity' (1978: 252). And yet one is experientially in touch with a great pool of constancies and steady processes of change in one's environment – which includes one's own body, of which one is almost constantly aware, however thoughtlessly, both by external sense and by proprioception. If one does not reflect very hard, these constancies and steadinesses of development in the *contents* of one's consciousness may seem like fundamental characteristics of the *operation* of one's consciousness, although they are not. This in turn may support the sense of the *mental self* as something truly uninterrupted and continuous throughout the waking day. And this in turn may smooth the path to the idea of the mental self, rather than just the human being considered as a whole, as an entity that may be continuous during sleep, and so from week to week to month to year.

I'm not claiming that belief in the flow of consciousness is *necessary* to a sense of the mental self as something that has long-term continuity. One could think that consciousness was gappy and chaotic and still believe in a mental self that had such continuity. An already established belief in the continuous mental self could feed belief in the flowing nature of consciousness, rather than the other way about. All these things are possible. My suggestion is only that belief in the flow of consciousness may be one interesting and suspect source of support for a sense of the mental self as something that has long-term continuity.

For my part, I have no sense of seamless flow or continuity in the *process of consciousness*. As just remarked, it doesn't immediately follow that I have no sense of the continuing *mental self*. And when one first tries to think about one's sense of the mental self – and to think about it, rather than simply have it, is already a difficult thing to do – one's first reaction may well be that it does present the mental self as a single continuing thing throughout the waking day: something that *has* all the interrupted and jumping thoughts and experiences but is not itself a gappy interrupted thing. And doubtless this reaction draws on one's deep-set awareness that one is a diachronically continuous thing as an embodied human being, and on a similarly deep-set background awareness of a distinctively mental continuity: the fact that one has, as a human being, a continuing and consistent personality, or, at the very least, a robustly persisting body of basic beliefs, preferences, mental abilities, and so on.

In my case, however, this first reaction is weak, and soon undermined. As I think further about my mental life, I'm met by the sense that there is no 'I' or self that goes on through the waking day (and beyond), even though there is an 'I' or self at any given time. And this is a report of experience, not a statement of a theoretical position. I feel I have continuity through the waking day only as an embodied human being. If I consider myself specifically as a mental subject of experience, my sense is that I am continually new.

When I say 'new', I don't mean new or different in respect of personality and outlook. I have an adequate grasp of the similarities that characterize me from day to day when I'm considered as an embodied human being. So considered, I am happy to agree that I am a single subject of experience with long-term continuity. But when I consider the fundamental experience of myself as a mental self, my deep feeling is that I am continually new, that I am always, in Updike's words, 'just beginning'. The experience of the 'I' as in *some* sense new each time is (I suggest) fundamental and universal, although it is occluded by familiar and contrary habits of thought, and may emerge clearly only on reflection. I feel I am a nomad in time, although the metaphor is intussusceptive, because it is the 'I' itself that has the transience of abandoned camping grounds.

I don't think that the brevity of the 'conscious now' necessarily contributes to the sense of hiatus or newness, for one's experience could resemble a narrow beam of light sweeping smoothly along. The length of the conscious now may set an upper bound on hiatus-free periods of thought, but it certainly doesn't follow that there will always be conscious experience of hiatus within any four-second waking period (in some people, there may be none for days). Nor, crucially, am I claiming that the mental self will never appear to last longer than the conscious now, when duly reflected on. My use of the word 'long-term' is vague but not idle: the self can certainly be felt to persist throughout a period of time that includes a break or hiatus, and its temporal extent may appear very different in different contexts of thought (fear of death raises interesting questions). It may well be impossible for human beings to function with no sense at all of the diachronic continuity of the self. The present challenge is only addressed to anything that purports to be a sense of the *long-term* continuity of the self.

Some may doubt my claims about how I experience consciousness; those who do not may think I'm part of a small minority. Experience like mine may be thought to be the unnatural result of philosophy, or drugs. But even if the experience of disjunction did result specifically from philosophical reflection, it wouldn't follow that it resulted from philosophy distorting the data. Philosophy may simply make one examine the already existing nature of one's experience more closely. Even if the experience were unnatural or uncommon in daily life, it would not follow that it gives a less accurate picture of how things are; for many natural experiences represent things inaccurately. More importantly, the experience may be natural in the sense that any ordinary human being who considers the matter will find that they come to have it.

8   To conclude. I've argued that one can have a clear and vivid sense of the mental self, at any particular time, without having any sense of it as something that has personality. I've also argued that one may have such a sense of the mental self without experiencing the supposed self as something that has long-term continuity. I've suggested that this is not just an abstract possibility, but a human reality. This claim may seem alien and implausible to those who live narratively; for others it is natural.[10]

Does this improve the prospects for the claim that a sense of the mental self could be an accurate representation of something that actually exists, and that exists even if materialism is true? I think it does, although the full argument would require a very careful statement of what it is to be a true materialist, further enquiry into the notion of a thing, and a challenge to the scientifically problematic distinction between things and processes. Perhaps the best account of the existence of the self is one that may be given by certain Buddhists. It allows that a mental self exists, at any given moment, but it retains all the essential Buddhist criticisms of the idea of the self, and gives no reassurance to those who believe in the (non-physical) soul. So it takes us from soul to self. But it doesn't leave us with nothing: it stops short of the view defended by many analytic philosophers, according to which the mental self is a myth in so far as it is thought to be different from the human being considered as a whole. It leaves us with what we have, at any given time – a self that is materialistically respectable, distinctively mental, and as real as a stone.

Notes

1 This distinction is related to, but distinct from, Wittgenstein's flawed distinction between the use of 'I' 'as object' and the use 'as subject' (1958: 65–8).
2 It may be added that there are striking cases – e.g. bodily acts of sexual love, and intense intellectual conversations – in which, in a very strong sense, we naturally relate to each other as mental selves. For a related thought about the sexual case, see Strawson 1991: 166n.
3 I suspect that we are especially likely to do this if we are preoccupied with our bodies, rather than less likely. Fichte does not disagree when he says that 'the majority of men could sooner be brought to believe themselves a piece of lava in the moon than to take themselves for a *self*' (1794–1802: 162), for he has something very special in mind.
4 Russell Hurlburt made random samplings of the character of people's experience as they went about their daily life by activating beepers that they carried with them: 'it was striking that the great majority of subjects at the time of the beep were focused on some inner event or events, with no direct awareness of outside events at that moment' (Hurlburt *et al.* 1994: 387). It is instructive to watch people in the street.
5 Strawson (1959: 101–10). I use 'non-mental' where others use 'physical' because I am a materialist and hold that everything that exists is physical. Consequently I hold that all mental phenomena are physical phenomena (including the qualitative phenomena of conscious experience *considered just as such*), and that mental phenomena cannot be opposed to physical phenomena. The real opposition is between mental and non-mental phenomena.
6 Remember that my claim is that even consistent and thoughtful materialists do this, and that it does not involve any belief that anything non-physical exists.
7 For a sustained criticism of the relativist position from the point of view of evolutionary psychology, see Cosmides and Tooby (1992).
8 When one is alone and thinking, one may also be walking, cycling, or running. Strenuous or complicated physical activity – or pain – need not lessen the sense of the mental self's independence of the body. On the whole, it is more likely to increase it.

9 This is Richardson's Miriam Henderson in church: 'Certainly it was wrong to listen to sermons . . . stultifying . . . unless they were intellectual . . . lectures like Mr Brough's . . . that was as bad, because they were not sermons . . . Either kind was bad and ought not to be allowed . . . a homily . . . sermons . . . homilies . . . a quiet homily might be something rather nice . . . and have not *Charity* – sounding brass and tinkling cymbal . . . *Caritas* . . . I have *none* I am sure . . . ' (1979: 73). Compare Molly Bloom in bed: 'I want to do the place up someway the dust grows in it I think while Im asleep then we can have music and cigarettes I can accompany him first I must clean the keys of the piano with milk what'll I wear a white rose or those fairy cakes in Liptons at 7½d a lb or the other ones with the cherries in them and the pinky sugar 11d a couple of lbs of those a nice plant for the middle of the table Id get that cheaper in wait wheres this I saw them not long ago I love flowers . . . ' (1986: 642). And Stephen Daedalus walking on the beach: 'Who watches me here? Who ever anywhere will read these written words? Signs on a white field. Somewhere to someone in your flutiest voice. The good bishop of Cloyne took the veil of the temple out of his shovel hat: veil of space with coloured emblems hatched on its field. Hold hard. Coloured on a flat: yes, that's right' (1986: 40).

10 Narrative personalities may feel there is something chilling and empty in the Episodic life. They may fear it, and judge that it shows lack of wisdom, conduces to lack of moral responsibility, and is 'deficient and empty' (Plutarch 1939: 217). This, however, is ignorance: even in its extreme form this life is no less intense or full, no less emotional and moral.

References

Berkeley, G. (1975), *Philosophical Works*, ed. M. R. Ayers (London: Dent).

Collins, S. (1982), *Selfless Persons* (Cambridge: Cambridge University Press).

Cosmides, L., and Tooby, J. (1992), 'The psychological foundations of culture', in Jerome Barkow, Leda Cosmides and John Tooby (eds), *The Adaptive Mind* (New York: Oxford University Press).

Dennett, D. (1991), *Consciousness Explained* (Boston: Little, Brown).

Fichte, J. G. (1982), *The Science of Knowledge,* ed. and trans. P. Heath and J. Lachs (Cambridge: Cambridge University Press).

Glover, J. (1988), *I: The Philosophy and Psychology of Personal Identity* (Harmondsworth: Penguin).

Holub, M. (1990), *The Dimension of the Present Moment* (London: Faber).

Hopkins, G. M. (1959), *Sermons and Devotional Writings*, ed. C. J. Devlin (London: Oxford University Press).

Hume, D. (1978), *A Treatise of Human Nature*, ed. L. A. Selby-Bigge and P. H. Nidditch (Oxford: Oxford University Press).

Hurlburt, R., Happé F., Frith, U. (1994), 'Sampling the form of inner experience in three adults with Asperger syndrome', in *Psychological Medicine*, 385–95.

James, W. (1950), *The Principles of Psychology,* vol. I (New York: Dover).

James, W. (1984), *Psychology: Briefer Course* (Cambridge, Mass.: Harvard University Press).

Joyce, J. (1986), *Ulysses* (Harmondsworth: Penguin).

Plutarch, (1939), 'On tranquillity of mind', in Plutarch, *Moralia*, vi, trans. W. C. Helmbold (Cambridge, Mass.: Harvard University Press).

Pöppel, E. (1978), 'Time perception', in R. Held, H. W. Leibovitz, and H. L. Teuber (eds.), *Handbook of Sensory Physiology* (New York: Springer).

Richardson, D. (1979), *Pointed Roofs, Pilgrimage* (London: Virago Press).

Ruhnau, E. (1995), 'Time gestalt and the observer', in T. Metzinger (ed.), *Conscious Experience* (Thorverton: Imprint Academic).

Strawson, G. (1991), *Freedom and Belief,* revised edn (Oxford: Clarendon Press).

Updike, J. (1989), *Self-Consciousness* (London: Deutsch).

Wittgenstein L. (1953), *Philosophical Investigations* (Oxford: Blackwell).

Wittgenstein L. (1958), *The Blue and Brown Books* (Oxford: Blackwell).

SELECT BIBLIOGRAPHY

Barnes, J. (1987) *Early Greek Philosophy*, London: Penguin Books.

Blackburn, S. (1994) *The Oxford Dictionary of Philosophy*, Oxford, Oxford University Press.

Blakemore, C. and Greenfield, S. (eds) (1987) *Mindwaves. Thoughts on Intelligence, Identity and Consciousness*, Oxford: Basil Blackwell.

Bremmer, J. N. (1983) *The Early Greek Concept of the Soul*. 154pp. Princeton: Princeton University Press.

Churchland, P. S. (1988) *Matter and Consciousness: A Contemporary Introduction to the Philosophy of Mind*, Cambridge, Mass.: MIT Press.

Cornwell, J. (ed.) (1998) *Consciousness and Human Identity*, Oxford: Oxford University Press.

Cottingham, J. (1986) *Descartes*, Oxford: Blackwell Ltd.

Crick, F. (1994) *The Astonishing Hypothesis: The Scientific Search for the Soul*, London: Simon & Schuster.

Crick, F. and Koch, C. (1995) *Why Neuroscience May be Able to Explain Consciousness*. Scientific American 273: 84–5.

Cummins, D. D. and Allen, C. (eds) (1998) *The Evolution of Mind*, Oxford: Oxford University Press.

Dennett, D. (1991) *Consciousness Explained*, London: Allen Lane, the Penguin Press.

Freeman, M. (1993) *Rewriting the Self*, London: Routledge.

Grayling, A. C. (ed.) (1995) *Philosophy: A Guide through the Subject*, Oxford: Oxford University Press.

Honderich, T. (1993) *How Free Are You?* Oxford: Oxford University Press.

Kenny, A. (1989) *The Metaphysics of Mind*, Oxford: Oxford University Press.

Kenny, A. (1992) *What is Faith?* Oxford: Oxford University Press.

Körner, S. (1995) *Kant*, London: Penguin Books.

Martin, D. (1997) *Reflections on Sociology and Theology*, Oxford: Clarendon Press.

Radhakrishnan, S. and Moore, C. A. (1957) *A Sourcebook in Indian Philosophy*, Princeton: Princeton University Press.

Rosenthal, D. M. (ed.) (1991) *The Nature of Mind* New York: Oxford University Press.

Sandel, M. (1982) *Liberalism and the Limits of Justice*, Cambridge: Cambridge University Press.

Shand, J. (1993) *Philosophy and Philosophers*, UCL Press.

Strawson, P. (1992) *Analysis and Metaphysics; An Introduction to Philosophy*, Oxford: Oxford University Press.

Swinburne, R. (1986) *The Evolution of the Soul*, Oxford: Oxford University Press.

Taylor, C. (1992) *Sources of the Self*, Cambridge: Cambridge University Press.

Underwood, G. (ed.) (1982) *Aspects of Consciousness.* Vol. 3, *Awareness and self-Awareness*, London: Academic Press.

Warner, R., and Szubka, T. (eds.) (1994) *The Mind–Body Problem: A Guide to the Current Debate*, Oxford: Basil Blackwell.

Williams, B. (1973) *Problems of the Self*, Cambridge: Cambridge University Press.

——(1978) *Descartes: The Project of Pure Enquiry*, London: Penguin Books.

INDEX

155

Democritus 3
Descartes, René 6, 8–9, 11, 14–15, 40, 89–106, 110
desire 2, 8, 12–13, 60, 101–102
dianoia 16, 57, 61; *see also* mind
Dicaearchus 8, 10
Dionysius the Areopagite 57
dopamine 116, 121
DNA 100119–
dreams 78, 119–121
dualism 1, 6, 130, 137
Durkheim, Emile 130

ecstasy 72
Empedocles 9
Epicharmus 23
Epictetus 15, 17
Epiphanius of Salamis 51
essence 11, 23, 42, 74, 77, 82–83, 87, 93–94, 104
Eudemus 22
Evagrius of Pontus 60
Evodius 100
experience 2

form 20, 23–25, 33–34, 37, 42, 53, 58, 71–72, 77

Galen 10
God 21–22, 37, 49, 51–52, 54, 56, 58–59, 61, 63–64, 105
grace, divine 57, 59, 65–66
Greek Orthodox Church 4, 64, 70, 76
Gregory of Nyssa 49–50, 53, 56

heart 4, 56–59, 65–66, 81
Hegel, G. W. F. 2
Heidegger, Martin 143
Heraclitus 2, 18
Hesychasts 58
Hierocles 15–16
histamine 116
Homer 9–10, 17
Hopkins, Gerard Manley 40–42, 138
Hume, David 7, 40, 93, 135, 144, 147

Iamblichus 21
identity 21–22, 108; personal 22
image 49–51; divine 49, 51–52, 59, 63
immortality 10–11, 23; *see also* resurrection, immortal soul
intellect 13, 20, 34–39, 42–44, 54, 61, 66, 102; agent 35, 38; angelic 45; divine 45; receptive 35, 38, 44
Irenaeus of Lyons 51
Isaac of Nineveh (the Syrian) 65

Jung, Carl 59

Kant, Immanuel 15, 130, 145
Katha Upanishad 5–6

language 3, 21, 34–38, 47, 60, 70, 79–87, 90, 99–100, 102–106, 110, 126–150
Locke, John 15, 24
love 60, 126
Lucretius 24

Macarius the Egyptian 50, 53
maps 3, 4, 7
matter 24–25, 33–37
Maximus the Confessor 60–61
megethos 11
Menander 19
mind 1–2, 4, 7–8, 16, 46–47, 57, 84, 87, 90–93, 97–98, 104–106, 108–124, 126, 129–130; mind–body problem 2
Montaigne, Michel Eyquem de 14
mystery 4, 76

names 77, 79, 81–82
Nemesius of Emesa 50, 63
Neoplatonists 3, 10, 14, 21
neurons 109–117, 120–121
Nicene–Constantinopolitan creed 51–52, 54
Nikodimos of the Holy Mountain 62
noradrenaline 116
nous 20, 50, 54, 57, 61, 66; *see also* intellect